YOUR
SPIRIT ANIMAL
HELPERS

THE DIVINE GUARDIANS
OF YOUR HAPPINESS

Animal illustrations by Marc Brinkerhoff.
Photographic backgrounds by Phyllis Giarnese.
Digital composing by Marc Brinkerhoff and Phyllis Giarnese.

TABLE OF CONTENTS

PART ONE
HOW SPIRIT ANIMAL HELPERS CAN HELP
YOU CHANGE YOUR LIFE

Chapter One

Chapter Two

TABLE OF CONTENTS

Chapter Three

PART TWO
SPIRIT ANIMALS AND THEIR SPECIAL POWERS

Chapter Four

TABLE OF CONTENTS

Chapter Five

TABLE OF CONTENTS

Chapter Five (Continued)

PART ONE

HOW SPIRIT ANIMALS

CHANGE YOUR LIFE

CAN HELP YOU

CHAPTER ONE

What Are Spirit Animals?

Long ago, people believed that all things in heaven and earth were connected. They also understood that there is communication between all things in the natural world. Shamans still do. A *shaman* is a wise man or woman who is in touch with the forces of both the natural and the supernatural or spirit worlds and works with them for purposes of healing, protection, guidance, and gaining knowledge. Shamans have always lived in every culture the world over since before recorded time.

Animals have always played an integral role in our lives, but to the shaman, animals are more than just a source of food, companionship, transportation, or labor. They regard animals as teachers and messengers from the guides in the unseen realm, who can help us in our daily lives. Different animals embody their own special qualities and powers that they can lend us when we need them.

Although we have been taught that animals are lesser beings than humans, according to the world's indigenous cultures, this is not so. There is a great deal we can learn from animals. As you read this book, you'll discover the many ways animals in physical form and "spirit animals" residing in the invisible realm can help you and your loved ones.

EVERYONE HAS A SPIRIT ANIMAL

You have at least one spirit animal helper who is eager to be your guide and teacher. Some people think of spirit animals as similar to guardian angels or guides. Others view them as divine forces or energies that we can call on when the need arises. One Native American belief holds that spirit animals are physical animals who crossed over to the spirit realm when they died.

In pre-Christian Europe, some societies believed that the Divine Spirit took on a different animal form each year (as a bear one year, a deer another, etc.) as a way of interacting with the people. According to the shaman Kahuna masters of Hawaii and Polynesia, animal spirits live within us and lend us their unique characteristics, which influence our personalities and give us our special abilities. For instance, a champion runner might harbor the spirit of a cheetah inside, while a beaver spirit might reside in an architect.

TOTEMS

Perhaps you've heard of a "totem." Your personal totem is anything in nature with which you feel a strong affinity—an animal, bird, reptile, insect, or even a plant. A totem has special meaning for you. Some people refer to spirit animals as totem animals or power animals. These are all names for the same thing. Some Native American tribes carved totem poles to honor the animal deities that were especially important to them. During the Middle Ages, the Celts and other European clans performed similar acts when they fashioned crests or coats-of-arms with animal figures featured prominently in their designs and bore them proudly on their shields, banners, clothing, and other articles.

Regardless of how you perceive them, spirit animals are here to help us. You do not have to acknowledge or accept help from your spirit animal, though—it is your choice. Some people believe that your animal will continue to assist you regardless of whether or not you acknowledge its existence. Others say that if you reject your spirit animal, it will find somebody else who does want its help. By connecting with your animal helper and honoring it, however, you will benefit in countless ways—as you will see as you read on.

In Part Two, you'll meet thirty spirit animals, learn about their special characteristics, and discover the importance of these animals in your own life. All creatures great and small have unique powers and qualities.

ANIMAL DEITIES IN MANY TIMES AND CULTURES

Since the dawn of time, people around the world have understood the connection between the spirit realm and the creatures living on earth. Ancient paintings of animal-like beings, which appear to be gods and goddesses in animal form, are found on cave walls in many parts of the world. Paintings in the caves of Trois Frère and Lascaux, France, which date back to about 15,000 BC, are some of the most famous examples. Scholars believe they were created to solicit the animal deities' help in the hunt. Animal figurines have been excavated in archaeological digs throughout the world.

The world's religions, myths, legends, and stories are filled with spirit animals. Some gods and goddesses assume the forms of animals, birds, reptiles, or even mythical creatures like dragons and phoenixes. For example, the Norse god Odin (or Wodin) had two ravens as companions: Munin (memory) and Hugin (thought). In Eastern Europe, the Vila or forest fairies who protect the woodland creatures often appear in the shape of horses, swans, or snakes. Even people of Siberia believe each member of the tribe has a reindeer as a personal spirit guide to help them during this earthly existence. In Mexico, the nature god Quetzalcoatl is represented as a serpent, and the Australian Aborigines believe the Rainbow Serpent gave birth to them as a people.

The importance of spirit animals to the native peoples of North America is well known. As mentioned, tribes carved totem poles with images of animals and birds to honor the animal deities and invoke their powers. Medicine men and women often dressed in animal skins and feathers during ceremonies and danced to ask for blessings, protection, and assistance from their spirit animals. In these rituals, they sought to acquire the animal's power. Special animals were often encountered in vision quests. A vision quest is a time when your consciousness can travel into the spirit world to receive wisdom in the form of inner visions. (You'll read more about this in the next chapter.) Indian children were frequently given animal names.

White Buffalo Woman

The Plains Indians of the Lakota, Dakota, and Nakota tribes especially honor the White Buffalo Woman. This divine being, they say, first appeared at a time when there was much confusion and unrest among the people. She gave them several sacred objects and taught the different races how to live in harmony with each other–as well as with the members of the animal kingdom and the earth itself.

According to the Sioux's oral tradition, the White Buffalo Woman changed colors four times–from white to red to yellow to brown and back to white–symbolizing the four different races on earth. Then she promised to return to the people at the end of four ages.

In August of 1994, a rare white buffalo calf was born in Wisconsin. The chance of a buffalo being born white is about one in six billion. Many Native medicine men and women foresaw the birth of the white buffalo calf, who has been named Miracle. They believe she is the embodiment of the White Buffalo Woman. Interestingly, although Miracle was born white, her coat had turned yellow, red, and is now brown–just as White Buffalo Woman did.

Some Native Americans see the calf's birth as a sign giving hope to humanity during another period of confusion. They believe it is a reminder for us to live in harmony with one another and to respect the earth and all its inhabitants. The return of White Buffalo Woman, they say, also signals a coming age of rebirth, peace, and unity.

As you can see, spirit animals have been with us for eons. They are still with us.

THE INVISIBLE REALM WHERE SPIRIT ANIMALS LIVE

In indigenous cultures around the world, shamans journey into the spirit realm, which is sometimes referred to as "non-ordinary reality." (Our earthly world is known as "ordinary reality.") The spirit realm co-exists with our physical, earthly one and can be entered by those who have learned how to access it. This is the home of our spirit animal helpers.

Since the beings who dwell in the spirit realm don't have physical bodies, most people can't see them. However, we can communicate with them. At night, when we're asleep, we sometimes journey into the invisible realm to receive guidance from the spirit entities who live there. You can also travel there by means of your own "vision quest" or a "shamanic journey," which you'll learn more about in the next chapter.

Once you've met your spirit animal helper, you can talk with it during your ordinary, waking hours, too. Because spirit animals have much more highly developed senses than we do, they can hear us even if we can't hear or see them. Through awareness, knowledge, meditation and other attunement practices, you can expand your own awareness so that you'll be able to perceive the signals your spirit animal helper sends you. We'll talk about this more in Chapter Two.

As you forge your way through life, your spirit animal helpers will be there to guide you. You could think of them as "trailblazers" who will show you the way and give you encouragement when the way seems treacherous.

Connections Between Real Animals and Spirit Animals

There are many connections between physical animals and spirit animals. As mentioned above, some Native Americans believe spirit animals were once physical animals. Another view is that terrestrial animals are the agents of the spirit animals, and act as go-betweens bringing messages from the spirit world to us here on earth. Yet another theory holds that spirit animals enter the forms of earthly animals when they want to contact us. Some people also believe that certain physical animals can help us connect with our spirit animal guides.

While it may be impossible to prove the exact nature of the link between spirit animals and animals that share the earth with us, we know a strong connection does exist. We can see it in the special characteristics and powers that are common to both the physical animals and their spirit counterparts.

For example, birds spend most of their time in the air. Spiritual teachings tell us that the air element represents the mind and such things as heightened awareness, intellectual development, and wisdom. *Birds, as spirit helpers, can show you how to increase your mental powers and abilities.* Physical birds have exceptionally good vision. Therefore, spirit birds can help you to see things around you more clearly. Birds are also considered to be messengers of the spirit realm who can help raise your awareness to spiritual heights.

Terrestrial animals live on the earth. The earth element represents physical or material qualities. *As spirit animals, terrestrial creatures can help you handle matters related to work, money, health, and other practical concerns.*

Fish and other aquatic creatures live in water. The water element represent emotions, intuition, and creativity.

Therefore, spirit fish can assist you with relationships, self-expression, or developing psychic skills.

Some members of the animal kingdom, such as geese and beavers, are at home in more than one element. As spirit animals, they are especially good at helping you with complex matters, such as handling emotional stress that is affecting your physical health. They can also enable you to bridge any gulfs between the various aspects of your life.

Whenever you have a special need or interest, consider the attributes and characteristics of the different physical animals. (In Chapter Five, thirty animals and their corresponding "spirit beings" are described.) These will reveal the powers of the spirit animals and help you select the one(s) that can best help you with a concern.

PETS AS SPIRIT ANIMAL HELPERS

Although some Native Americans believe that only animals living in nature can become power animals, this view is not universally held. For many centuries, indigenous cultures have respected and worked with the divine qualities of domesticated animals.

Perhaps you've heard the term "familiar." While most people think a familiar is a witch's black cat, in actuality a familiar is any animal with whom you feel a strong, psychic affinity. It may be your pet collie, a blue jay who visits your bird feeder every day, or an animal you've never actually seen in the flesh, but which holds special significance for you.

A familiar has both physical and spirit qualities that can be used to assist you with healing, protection, and in countless other ways. (In Chapter Three, you'll read how pets and other animals have helped people just like you.)

If you think your pet may be your familiar, try to communicate with it without using your voice or other signals. Sit quietly and think about your pet. Call its name in your mind and ask it to come to you. Close your eyes and imagine your pet is at your side. Keep this up until your pet responds to your mental call. If you pet comes to your side, it is a good indication that s/he is your familiar or that you can begin to work with your pet in this manner.

When your pet looks at you as if it has something to tell you, try to sense what's on its mind. If your pet is indeed your familiar, you've probably already experienced this type of intuitive communication. The more you use it, the stronger and clearer it will become.

Not all pets are familiars, even though you may be very fond of them. All of us who have shared our lives with animal companions know that some are more special to us than others. You cannot force a pet to be your familiar—it must accept this role willingly. Let it freely choose to stay close to you and lend you its powers.

Animals can teach us how to open our hearts and love unconditionally. Animals also teach us to be true to ourselves and our own natures, just as they are true to their natures. A rabbit doesn't try to roar like a lion or soar like an eagle. Remember, you are part of nature. Your spirit animal can help you get to know this part of yourself and become the best "you" that you can be.

CHAPTER TWO

How to Find And Connect With Your Spirit Animal Helpers

B y now, you're probably curious about your spirit animal helper and eager to meet it. Perhaps you already have a particular fondness for a specific one. But just because you admire an animal doesn't mean it's your spirit animal helper, though it may visit you from time to time when you need its assistance.

SPIRIT ANIMALS CHOOSE US, WE DON'T CHOOSE THEM

If it were up to us, we might choose animals that look or behave in ways we find pleasing, rather than those representing qualities we need for different kinds of help, including personal and spiritual growth. In this chapter, you'll learn to recognize when your spirit animal is near and how to contact it when you want its help.

In working with spirit animal helpers, the most important thing is sincerity. Before your animal will reveal itself to you, you must truly want to meet it and ask it to appear to you. Here are some things you can do to get in touch with your spirit animal helper: Pay attention to little things. Be quiet. Slow down. Keep an open mind. Trust. Pray. Meditate. Ask your animal to come to you in a dream. Spend time in nature.

Don't give up hope if you don't succeed at first. Keep trying. Before long, your spirit animal helper will make itself known to you in a way that you will instantly understand.

HOW TO TELL WHEN YOUR SPIRIT ANIMAL IS NEAR

Usually you have one primary spirit animal, sometimes two. However, at different times when you need their help, various other animals may come into your life temporarily. Once you've made the connection with your primary animal, you can ask it to introduce you to other animals who have the power to help you with particular problems or situations.

Sometimes a spirit animal helper will show itself when it has a message for you. Sometimes they come to alert you to what's happening around you, or in times of urgency or need. Depending on the situation, an animal may come to you unbidden or you might have to ask it to appear. An animal won't present itself to you unless it is there to help you or has something to teach you.

As you become more familiar with spirit animals, you'll want to start keeping a journal of animal and bird sightings. It's also a good idea to keep a dream journal, recording all the animals who visit you while you're sleeping. The more you work with this information, the more useful it will be to you.

How Spirit Animals Make Themselves Known to Us

Spirit animal helpers make themselves known in various ways, depending on their natures, your ability to perceive them, and the circumstances at the time of their appearance.

Chuck's Story

Chuck's spirit animal helper is the butterfly. When he was a boy, he collected them and memorized the names and characteristics of hundreds of species. When he sits quietly in his yard, butterflies light on his body. Whenever something important is about to happen in his life, butterflies show up to guide him. When Chuck was making a major move, it was March in New England—not the usual season for butterflies. Yet as he carried furniture to the UHaul truck, a buckeye butterfly, which is rare in that part of the country, flew back and forth beside him. He felt it was giving its blessing to his move.

Here are some clues that may help you recognize your primary spirit animal:

⋆ **Do you feel a special affinity for a particular animal?** The writer Mark Twain was notoriously fond of cats. Whenever he was away from home for long periods of time, he rented cats from the local people to keep him company.

⋆ **Do you look like a particular animal or possess qualities that are distinctly associated with an animal?** Actor Roddy MacDowell, for example, looks a bit like a fox. Walter Matthau resembles a moose and Tony Randall a chipmunk.

⋆ **If you could transform yourself into an animal, which one would it be?**

⋆ **Does a certain animal appear to you frequently in your dreams?** Black Elk, the great Oglala medicine man, often dreamed of a bear that he credited with giving him the power to heal others.

⋆ **When you take a walk in nature or in the park, do you often see a certain animal?** In many indigenous cultures, the most respected animals are the ones that can be found nearby. For example, Native Americans revered bison and wolves; the Inuit Eskimos see polar bears and seals as their spirit animal helpers.

* *Are you afraid of any animals?* The Swiss psychiatrist C. G. Jung believed animals symbolize archetypes in the human consciousness. An animal you fear may represent your hidden or "shadow" side, a part of yourself that you dislike or don't acknowledge. By confronting this part and transforming it, you can make its energy work for you rather than against you. This is what the story of *Beauty and the Beast* is all about. After Beauty helped the Beast recognize his kind and gentle inner nature, he turned into the handsome prince, the personification of all his goodness.

Recognizing Animal Signs and Messages

Your primary spirit animal plays a different role than the other animal helpers who might appear to you from time to time. Your primary animal wants to develop a long-term relationship with you; ideally, it will be your guide for life. This animal can help you become stronger, healthier, happier, more balanced, and more productive. Other animal helpers enter your life as needed. They show you how to cope with specific problems or situations you are facing temporarily.

The messages spirit animals send you are not always obvious at first, but once you learn to speak their language you'll have no trouble reading their signs.

*Here are some clues that can help you begin to talk
with the animals:*

     * *Pay special attention to an animal that you don't usually
see, that is uncommon in your area or in an unusual place.*

Ellen's Story

Ellen is an independent career woman who had
never considered marriage. The first time she dated
Hugh, however, it was a dark and stormy night. As he
drove her home to her townhouse in metropolitan San
Francisco, a streak of lightning flashed to reveal a deer
standing in a vacant lot.

Deer symbolize gentleness. In this case, the deer
appeared to let Ellen know she could relax her guard and
open her heart to this man, who eventually became her
husband.

     * *An animal that appears in a dream is drawing your
attention to something specific in your life.* Adopting the
powers, behavior, or other traits of the animal can help you
cultivate or utilize your own energies in some way.

If an animal appears in a threatening manner, it can
mean that you are not utilizing or expressing the positive

qualities of the animal. For example, if a dog, who is considered "man's best friend," is snarling, this can indicate that you are not being friendly to someone who admires you.

    ⋆ *Study the animal's characteristics and traits.* Each animal has unique qualities and attributes, which you'll read more about in Chapter 5. These characteristics may be signals to you. For instance, a porcupine may be warning you to bolster your defenses, a snake to get ready for a change.

    ⋆ *What is the animal doing?* This may also be significant. If the animal is lying still, it may mean that you need to rest; if it's playing, you should lighten up and have some fun; if it's running away, you'd be wise to leave a situation behind.

    ⋆ *If the animal appears in a threatening manner or is unpleasant to you, is there something that this animal represents that you are avoiding, ignoring or overdoing?* For example, if ants have decided to set up residence in your home, perhaps you are not being as industrious as you might be regarding a specific matter. Or, perhaps you are being too industrious, compulsive, or over concerned about something. Armies of ants are famous for their ability to work until they have achieved their objectives. Are you working too hard or worrying too much about your job or about your future? According to shamanic tradition, it would be wise not to destroy the ants, but to try heeding their message. When you have successfully done so, they will move out on their own.

⋆ *How does the animal cope with its environment?*
This can suggest ways for coping with the demands in your
own life. For instance, a deer lies motionless in the woods,
fading into the background when it wants to elude the hunter.

⋆ *Note the animal's cycles.* Some animals are more
active at certain times of the day or night. Some hibernate,
migrate, change their appearance, or engage in certain
behaviors at particular times of the year. This could be
relevant to the animal's message. For instance, a squirrel
gathering nuts might suggest that the fall will be a busy time
for you or that you need to "squirrel away" some money.

⋆ *Is the animal alone or with others?* Sometimes more
than one animal will appear simultaneously. This may mean
that other people can assist you, or that you should combine
the characteristics of several animals to accomplish your aims.

⋆ *Notice the animal's movement.* If the animal is
coming toward you, you could add, increase, or develop
something in your life. An animal that is moving away can
indicate something should be reduced or eliminated.

⋆ *Who is the animal's prey or predator?* The two are
inexorably linked and their characteristics combine to create
balance. Are you afraid of the qualities represented by the
animal's predator? Have you ever feared gossip by someone
who's "catty"? Do you lack respect for the qualities
represented by its prey? Were you ever the "scared rabbit"?

CONTACTING YOUR SPIRIT ANIMAL

Now it's time to meet your personal spirit animal. You may meet it in a dream, a vision quest, or some other way. When you do, you'll know that this is your special guide and helper, and that it will always be there whenever you want its assistance or companionship.

Whether you meet your spirit animal helper in the shape of a physical animal, or in a dream or other vision, it will be pleasant and approach you directly. It will not sneak up and startle you. It will never bite, scratch, sting, bare its fangs, growl at you, or harm you in any way. It won't frighten, chase, or attack you in a dream.

If your first contact with the animal should happen to be frightening, before you decide that this is not your own power animal, think about whether or not its negative approach may be for a reason. The reason might be such as that talked about with the threatening dog or the pesky ants. If after thinking over a possible message for you, and maybe acting on the advice you perceive, the animal's next contact is still a negative experience, then the animal probably is not your spirit animal helper. Your spirit animal is your friend and your meetings with it will always be positive.

If you should encounter negative behavior from an animal during a dream, vision quest, shamanic journey, or mental visualization, ignore that animal, unless you find a message in its unpleasant behavior toward you. Pass it by or command it to leave.

As mentioned, the most important prerequisite to meeting your animal is a sincere desire to do so. If the animal does not simply present itself to you of its own accord, ask it to do so and continue asking until it does.

Preparing to Meet Your Animal Guide

As you prepare to meet your spirit animal helper, remember to keep an open mind. Don't hold any preconceptions about which animal is your special helper. Don't hold any expectations of how the animal will come to you. Don't try to force anything–let it happen naturally, in its own time.

Here are some ways you can begin to demonstrate your desire to meet your spirit animal helper:

* Watch animal or nature shows on TV.

* Look at pictures of animals in books (even children's books) and wildlife calendars.

* Visit a zoo or farm.

* Watch animals in your yard, a park, or other outdoor area.

* Read books, especially children's stories, about animals such as *Black Beauty, Bambi, The Yearling,*

The Black Stallion, or *Lassie.* In these stories, the animal champions teach the human characters the qualities of love, compassion, and hope.

EXERCISES AND TECHNIQUES FOR FINDING YOUR SPIRIT ANIMAL

Here are some other techniques you can use to find your spirit animal helper:

⋆ *Dreaming.* Before you fall asleep at night, ask your spirit animal to make itself known to you in a dream. When it does, pay attention to what it says or does—it has come to give you guidance or help.

⋆ *Scrying.* This is similar to what clairvoyants do when they gaze into a crystal ball. Begin by quieting your mind through meditation, breathing exercises, or another relaxation method. (For example: Close your eyes and begin breathing slowly in a rhythmic manner, inhaling to a count of four, then holding your breath for a count of four, then exhaling to a count of four; repeat this cycle five times. Or, you might prefer to imagine the way your breath looks as it enters and leaves your body.) Put the rational, questioning part of your mind on hold and let your imagination flow. Gaze calmly in a pool of water or another dark, shiny surface such as a piece of smoked glass or polished sheet of metal.

Gradually, your own face may grow fuzzy and start to take on characteristics that you associate with a particular animal. Or, you may see the image of an animal slowly emerge behind or beside you. When this happens, you may feel the animal's power enter you. Now ask the animal what information it may have for you or how it can help you. You may "hear" it speak to you in your mind or you may simply intuit the animal's response.

⋆ *Watching clouds.* When you were a child, you may have made a game of watching clouds shift and change into recognizable shapes. Lie on your back and let your childlike imagination soar once again. Watch the clouds and see what animal shapes they take. As you recognize their forms, begin to communicate mentally with the animals you see. You may want to ask them to help you with a special question or problem; or you might simply lie quietly and listen to what they have to share with you.

⋆ *Visualizing.* Go to a special place where you won't be disturbed–preferably somewhere out-of-doors. Sit quietly, close your eyes, and calm your mind through meditation, breathing exercises, or another relaxation method. You may choose to set the mood by listening to soothing music or to beating softly and rhythmically on a small drum. Allow your imagination to unfold and express itself freely.

While in the meditative state with your eyes closed, envision a dense, green forest before you. Walk toward these sacred woods and enter them. Feel the cool shade on your shoulders and smell the fragrant scents of the plants around you. Continue walking deeper and deeper into the woods until you come to a lovely clearing. Wait here quietly, enjoying the pleasant sounds and smells of the forest.

In a few moments, you see an animal emerging from the greenery and moving toward you. As it comes closer, you recognize it as your spirit animal helper. Greet it warmly and thank it for coming to meet you. If you want, you can reach out to touch it gently. Ask it if it wants to tell you something. You may hear its response, or you may simply sense what it is communicating to you. Spend as much time with your spirit animal as you wish.

When you are ready to return to your ordinary, waking consciousness, say "so long" to your animal helper and promise to meet again soon. Watch your animal slip back into the forest, then retrace your steps out of the forest. When you open your eyes, you'll feel rested, rejuvenated, and at peace. You can repeat this visualization exercise anytime you want to visit with your animal guide. Be sure to record in a notebook what occurred.

* *Shamanic Journey.* In your mind, go to a place in nature where you feel safe and happy. It could even be in a city. Now find an opening in the earth–it could be at the base of a tree, behind a rock, an underwater cavern, or whatever comes to mind. Mentally enter this opening and feel yourself crawling or walking through a tunnel beneath

the earth until you emerge into a setting in nature. (This, too, can be someplace in a city.)

When you come out of the tunnel, you see your spirit animal waiting there for you. Watch what it does. Listen as it speaks to you telepathically. Ask its name. Follow if it leads you somewhere. If you don't immediately spot an animal waiting for you, begin to explore the area. Walk around and see if there is an animal in the area. When you come upon one, ask if it is your spirit animal helper. If it says no, ask it to take you to your animal. When you meet your spirit animal, ask if it has something to tell you. Listen intuitively to what it says.

Spend as much time as you like communicating with your animal. When you are ready to leave, retrace the path you took to reach this spot, knowing that you can come back again whenever you want. Record these journeys. They are like dreams and will fade if you don't capture them while they're fresh in your mind.

Honoring Your Spirit Animal

Once you've met your spirit animal helper, you may want to honor it.

Here are some ways to show your thanks and respect for the help you receive from your spirit animal:

* Collect pictures, figurines, et cetera of your animal.

* Wear jewelry or clothing decorated with its image.

* Draw pictures of it or fashion its image in stone, clay, wood, or other material.

* Donate money or volunteer to work for a cause that helps/protects your animal or its relatives.

What Happens if Your Spirit Animal Leaves?

Sometimes a spirit animal doesn't return after its mission is accomplished. In such a case, another one is likely to come to you when needed or called upon. Perhaps you've behaved in a way that has offended your spirit animal, such as not being as kind as you could to a physical animal. Without the guidance and assistance of your spirit animal helper, you may feel somewhat at a loss. You may not be able to do as well on your own. So, it's important to learn how to trust your animal. Perhaps you've ignored or rejected your spirit animal's help. Shamanic tradition holds that when a spirit animal leaves you because it is unhappy for some reason, your luck can begin to turn against you.

Susan's Story

Susan was house-hunting and found one she liked that was very reasonably priced. When she asked her spirit animal if she should buy it, however, he told her no. But Susan ignored her animal's advice. Soon after Susan moved into her new home, the trouble started. The roof leaked after a big rainstorm and the basement filled up with several inches of water. Next she discovered that the electrical wiring had been done incorrectly, so that she couldn't use her oven and clothes dryer at the same time. Over the next three months, Susan encountered one annoying–and costly–problem after another. Finally, Susan petitioned her spirit animal for help by following the practices described below. A week later, she "accidentally" met two men at the paint store: one was a carpenter, the other an electrician. They began talking and soon agreed to work with Susan. Before long, the two men had taken care of the problems in her home–and at a price she could afford. Today, Susan lives comfortably in her home, and she is grateful to her spirit animal for sending her the two men who set things right.

How to Bring A Lost Animal Helper Back

If your luck has been going downhill, it's possible your spirit animal helper has chosen to leave for one reason or another. However, spirit animals are more patient and forgiving than people and if they see that you truly desire their help, they'll return.

*Here are some things you can do to show your
sincerity and bring your spirit animal helper back:*

* If your spirit helper is a bird, build a bird house for
  its physical representatives here on earth.

* Put out food for your spirit animal helper and for
  other hungry animals.

* If your spirit helper is an insect, such as a bee or
  butterfly, plant special flowers to attract it.

* Donate money to a wildlife protection organization
  or animal rights group.

* Volunteer your time to help wild, stray, or injured
  animals.

* Adopt a pet from a shelter or pound.

* Avoid buying products made from wild animals or
  endangered species.

* Shun products from companies that do animal
  testing. Look for the cruelty-free symbol on
  cosmetics and personal care items.

* Do a shamanic journey, like the one previously
  described, to reconnect with your spirit
  animal helper.

* Native Americans and other indigenous people only

*hunt birds and animals for food, not for sport. If
you eat the meat of an animal, remember to thank it
for its willing sacrifice.*

These are only a few suggestions—you'll probably think of others. The point is to demonstrate respect and consideration for the creatures here on earth who are the representatives of our spirit animal helpers, as well as for the spirit animals themselves.

Now let's consider some of the ways spirit animals have helped other people and can help you, too.

CHAPTER THREE

How Spirit Animals Can Help You

Your spirit animal helper always has your best interests at heart and will gladly come to your aid if asked. If your animal helper cannot assist you with a particular matter, it will lead you to another animal who can.

Through your primary spirit animal, you can connect with and draw on the power of the entire spirit animal kingdom. It's good to have a variety of helpers to assist you with the many different tasks, challenges, problems, and situations that you face as you move through life. Since each animal has unique powers and attributes, you can call upon the one best suited to your specific needs or situation at any given time.

Here are some of the many ways spirit animal guides have helped others and can help you too.

PROTECTION

Charlene's Story

For several months, Charlene had been stalked by a man she had never met. He left threatening messages on her telephone answering machine and sent her obscene letters. Often he parked his truck outside the house where she lived alone and waited for her to come home from work. He even followed her when she ran errands or went shopping. On numerous occasions, Charlene called the police, but the man always left before they arrived. Unless he'd done something to actually harm her, the police claimed they could do nothing to protect her. Understandably, she was desperately beside herself with fear.

Then one day, Charlene learned about spirit animal helpers and turned to hers for assistance. In a guided meditation she met a sleek, powerful cheetah who promised to protect her.

When she received another terrifying message from the stalker, Charlene called the police again. This time, a woman officer named Detective Rohan came to talk with

Charlene. She was outraged at how the stalker had tormented Charlene. When the detective took off her jacket, she was wearing a tan blouse with black spots—Charlene knew immediately that she had been sent by the cheetah! Detective Rohan didn't give up until she'd caught the stalker, who it turned out was harassing other women as well. A terrible chapter in Charlene's life was ended, thanks to the aid of her spirit animal helper.

Spirit animals are always ready to protect you and your loved ones. They will also watch over and guard your home, car, pets, garden, or other precious possessions at your request. They have a special fondness for small children and domestic animals and can be called upon to keep them safe day and night, whether they are near or far away, especially when you cannot guard them yourself.

In some situations, as was the case with Charlene, your primary spirit helper and another animal who may be particularly well-adapted to handling the problem will work together on your behalf. If you want to protect a child or other loved one, your own spirit animal will often ally itself with that person's animal helper to keep your loved one safe.

How to Attract and Enhance the Spirit Animal's Power For Protection

To draw upon and enhance the protection you receive from your spirit animal helper, you can fashion an amulet similar to what Native Americans call a medicine bundle. Use a small pouch or bag made of natural material that is colored blue. In it place feathers/fur from your bird/animal totem or a bird/animal whose power you wish to invoke to protect you. (Do not harm the bird or animal in order to obtain these. If you seek them in earnest, you'll find them or they will be brought to you.) If you can't find a small piece of fur or feathers, an image of the bird or animal taken from a magazine or hand-drawn, a carving, or a piece of jewelry will do.

Next, add a piece of quartz crystal or a stone noted for its protective qualities, such as jade, turquoise, amber, or topaz. Finally, put in some protective herbs and/or dried flowers, such as snapdragon, ash bark or leaf, star anise, pussy willow, fennel, thyme, peony seeds, verbena, or chamomile. Carry the pouch in your pocket or purse at all times and sleep with it under your pillow to protect you, when and if you feel the need.

Problem-Solving

Vicki's Story

Vicki had always been fascinated with elephants. When she was a child, her favorite story was *Dumbo* and she had a collection of stuffed elephants that were her most cherished toys. She loved to visit the elephants at the zoo and begged her parents to take her to see them as often as possible. Even in adulthood, Vicki retained her affection for the great creatures and wore a small jade carving of an elephant on a chain around her neck.

Vicki had been working for an international airline for several years when a new boss was hired. For some reason, he took an instant dislike to Vicki and assigned her to the most stressful tasks, the most tiresome shifts, plus harshly criticized her work, and generally made her job miserable. Although Vicki liked most aspects of her job, she feared she would have to quit because of her boss.

Then one day at the ticket counter, Vicki met a man from India who noticed her elephant necklace and told her about the Hindu god Ganesh. This elephant-headed deity, he said, lends its tremendous strength to people and helps them overcome formidable obstacles or adversaries. Touching the tiny jade elephant, Vicki silently wished for a solution to her problem.

The next morning when she arrived at the airline, Vicki learned that her boss was being transferred to another location. She was certain the elephant had played a part in this change of events. Vicki now knows that she can call on the power of Ganesh, her spirit animal helper, whenever she is faced with a dilemma that is too big for her to handle alone.

We all encounter problems regularly, both small and monumental ones. In Chapter Five, you'll learn about the special powers of various animals who can help you resolve your difficulties. Study the attributes associated with the earthly animals to see which traits you can assume yourself when you need them, or which animals you can call upon in the spirit form to help you.

How to Attract and Enhance the Spirit Animal's Power For Problem Solving

You can fashion your own animal image or "fetish" to assist you in times of trouble. Depending on your skill level and preference, you can create your fetish from clay, stone, wood, cloth, glass, wax, or metal. It can be realistic or stylized. You may also choose to paint it with magical symbols. You can even incorporate feathers or fur from the bird or animal. Decide which spirit animal helper is best suited to help you in your particular situation (see Chapter Five), then make a miniature likeness of that animal.

Clear your mind of any negative thoughts or doubts before you begin. Then as you work on your fetish, affirm aloud that this spirit animal guardian is already helping you overcome your problem. Carry your fetish with you whenever you need some extra help or put it in a place where you will see it often (your desk or coffee table, for example). Each time you see or touch this symbol, you'll be reminded of the spirit animal's power and know that it is working to help you.

GUIDANCE

Daisy's Story

Years ago, Daisy and her six-year-old son took a vacation to Florida to visit a friend. Their flight was delayed and didn't arrive until nearly midnight. Rather than ask her friend to drive to the airport to pick them up so late, Daisy rented a car and set out for her friend's home. After an hour of driving, Daisy realized she had made a wrong turn somewhere and was now hopelessly lost on dark, deserted back roads. There were no gas stations where she could ask directions. Tired and beginning to panic, she was close to tears.

It was at this point that Daisy noticed the odor of skunk wafting through the car window. Suddenly she recalled a psychic reading she'd had a few months earlier in which an elderly Native American medicine woman told her that her spirit animal helper was a skunk. This rang a bell for Daisy, who strangely had always loved the skunk's pungent odor. She immediately sensed that her skunk guide was there to help her. Soon Daisy came to an intersection and "just knew" to turn left. In a few minutes, she spotted an all-night diner. There she was able to call her friend, who drove to the diner and led Daisy and her son back to the house.

Now, whenever Daisy feels lost–either physically or when she is confused about which direction to take in her personal or professional life–she turns to her skunk helper for guidance. It has led her to the right doctor in times of illness, given her wisdom in raising her son, and assisted her in numerous other ways. She never feels alone; her spirit animal is always there.

Because a spirit animal's vision is not limited in the way ours is, spirit animal helpers can see in every direction, far beyond what our physical eyes could possibly perceive. They can even gaze into the invisible realms and the future. As a result, they are well equipped to guide us when we can't find our way alone. They even know what's best for us when we don't know ourselves. Like a lighthouse, our spirit animal helpers can lead us across the stormy seas of life to a safe harbor.

Once you've made the initial connection with your primary spirit animal helper, start a scrapbook to honor the animal. Collect pictures of the animal's earthly counterpart from magazines, books, postcards, stamps, etc. and paste them in your scrapbook. You may also want to draw portraits of your spirit animal as you perceive it. In addition, keep notes of the ways your animal helper has guided you through difficult situations. Each time you add a new picture or write down a new experience, you reinforce the connection between you and your spirit animal. Whenever you need its guidance, you can open your scrapbook and be reassured that your special helper will show you the way.

HEALING

Tom's Story

Tom is a single man in his late twenties who shares his home with two cats, a large black-and-white male and a gray tabby female. One morning he fell sick with a high fever and intense chest pains. The illness came upon him so suddenly and unexpectedly that he wasn't even able to get to a doctor. He only had enough strength to crawl into bed. His two cats promptly climbed up on the bed and situated themselves on either side of Tom, purring loudly.

For three days and nights, Tom's illness raged. He was so weak and feverish he couldn't even phone anyone for help. But help came to him anyway–in the shape of his two feline friends. Throughout those painful three days and nights, Tom's cats kept their vigil on his bed. They literally never left his side. At times, he had the odd sensation that they were drawing the illness out of him. Finally, Tom's fever broke and the pains in his chest subsided. The cats seemed to know he was out of danger, because they licked his face, then jumped down and went to find something to eat.

Tom is convinced that his cats healed him, maybe even saved his life. Since then he's noticed that whenever he's feeling bad, physically or emotionally, they come to comfort him. They seem to sense when something is wrong and won't leave him alone until he's better. Whenever he's tense or worried, Tom finds that just stroking his cat companions makes him feel calmer. And each time he looks into their mysterious yellow-green eyes, he can almost see another, a spiritual presence there within.

Many of us who live with animal pets are aware of their great sensitivity and compassion. They seem to be able to read our emotional and physical states, and even appear to be psychic at times. Have you ever thought about opening a can of pet food and noticed your dog was right at your feet–before you'd even taken the food out of the cabinet? And even if you've never had an experience as dramatic as Tom's, you've probably felt the special sense of serenity you get from being with your pet; holding your cat on your lap or taking a walk with your dog. As you read in Chapter One, our pet companions are often the physical representatives of our spirit animal helpers. Treat them with kindness and respect, and they will care for you in innumerable ways.

How to Attract and Enhance the Spirit Animal's Power For Healing

Shamans often wear the skins, feathers, teeth, and claws of their totem animals in order to attract the animals' powers into their own bodies. By imitating your animal helper you, too, can call upon its power to heal your body, mind, or spirit. Either purchase or create a mask in the image of your animal guide. You may want to incorporate actual feathers or fur into your mask. If you prefer, you can paint your face so that it resembles your animal's. "Dance" your spirit animal's dance by moving your body the way the animal might: hop if your spirit animal helper is a rabbit; roar and walk about proudly on all fours if your animal is a lion; flap your arms and chirp if you have a bird totem. Let yourself become one with your spirit animal helper. Feel the animal's power entering and healing your body.

FINDING LOST ITEMS

Dennis's Story

Dennis had lost his watch. It wasn't an expensive watch, but it had belonged to his deceased grandfather and held tremendous sentimental value for him. He'd looked everywhere he could think to look for it, but without success. Crestfallen, he was about to give up.

Then one afternoon he was out in the yard when he spied a pheasant. In his suburban neighborhood, a pheasant was a rare bird indeed. Fascinated, he slowly approached the pheasant. To his surprise, it didn't fly off, but instead waited until he was only a few steps away, then hopped out of reach. Once more Dennis moved slowly toward the bird and again it remained on the ground until he was very close before scurrying along. Several times, Dennis and the pheasant repeated this "game." Finally the pheasant came to the edge of the flower garden. This time, when Dennis approached it, the bird flew away.

Sadly, Dennis watched until the pheasant was out of sight. The wild bird had seemed so tame, he almost hoped it might decide to stick around and become a pet. Then Dennis happened to glance down at the garden. There, shining beneath the leaves of a lily, was his watch! The strap had broken while he was weeding the flower bed and the watch had fallen off unnoticed. The pheasant had led him to it!

Sometimes when we lose an item, the memory of the incident remains in the subconscious mind. In these cases, our spirit animal helpers can enable us to remember where we misplaced the object. But other times, we have no way of knowing where the lost thing is; for instance, when it is in the possession of another person. In situations like this, spirit animals' special, unlimited sight lets them see where we cannot. The next time you lose something, ask your animal helper to lead you to it. Wait until you sense a signal, as if you are being drawn in a particular direction, then go with your impressions. Trust your intuition—that's often how spirit animal helpers speak to us. Or, ask your animal to show you where the lost item is, perhaps in a vision, meditation, or dream.

How to Attract and Enhance the Spirit Animal's Power For Possessions

Always pay close attention to the way animals and birds communicate, with each other and with us. Watch animals in the park, the woods, your own home. Listen closely to a bird's song, a dog's bark, a squirrel's chatter. Try to still your mind and emotions, and open up to the animal. Can you understand what it's saying? Can you sense whether it's happy, angry, frightened? If you live with an animal, try to communicate intuitively with it. Instead of calling aloud, *mentally* ask it to come to you or envision it at your side. How often does it work? When your pet looks at you, try to understand what it's attempting to tell you. The more aware you become of the natural world and the more attuned you become to the creatures in it, the more easily it will be to benefit from the help they offer.

SEEING INTO THE FUTURE

Joan's Story

Joan wanted very much to find a man with whom she could have a lasting and fulfilling relationship. She'd tried blind dates, dating services, even answering personal ads in the newspaper, but she hadn't met "Mr. Right" yet. Finally she decided to ask her spirit animal to help her.

Joan's spirit animal helper is a hawk, a bird known for its keen vision. Joan took an imaginary "spirit journey" with her hawk to see into her future. She felt as though she was riding on the hawk's back as she flew forward in time. Looking down, she could see the earth below whizzing by.

Suddenly the hawk swooped low enough for Joan to spot herself. She was surrounded by people in a crowded exhibition hall. It appeared to be some sort of convention. From the hawk's back, Joan watched as the man standing beside her on the convention floor bumped into her, accidentally knocking her cup of coffee out of her hand. He apologized profusely and offered to buy her another cup. She accepted and as they made their way to the cafeteria, Joan "just knew" this was the man she'd been looking for! She tried to read his name badge, but all she could see was the letter R. How in the world was she going to find him?

Several weeks after going on the journey with her hawk, Joan came across an announcement in a magazine of an upcoming conference being held in a nearby city. As she gazed at the advertisement, Joan's heart started to flutter and she felt certain this was what she had seen in her journey. Immediately, Joan phoned the number listed in the ad and ordered a ticket.

As soon as she set foot in the convention hall, Joan had a powerful sense of déjà vu. It was exactly as she'd seen it from the hawk's back. Joan bought a cup of coffee, then took a few deep breaths, envisioned her spirit animal helper perched on her shoulder, and allowed herself to be led down the crowded aisles.

She had finished about half her coffee when she was jostled from behind. The cup fell from her hand. Suddenly, a man in a gray suit was beside her, apologizing and offering her his handkerchief. Ordinarily, Joan might not have noticed him–he seemed quiet and scholarly, rather than the rugged, athletic type Joan usually found attractive. But when she spotted the name "Roger" on his conventioneer's badge, she knew he was the one. Joan and Roger hit it off immediately and were married four months later. They are expecting their first child soon, and sometimes

Joan is tempted to ask her spirit helper to show her whether it will be a boy or a girl, but then decides she'd rather wait and be surprised.

How to Attract and Enhance the Spirit Animal's Power For Viewing The Future

Do not eat or drink anything except water for at least an hour before beginning your visual journey into the future. Find a safe, quiet place where you can be completely alone and undisturbed. You may want to go to a place outdoors if weather and locale permit. If you are indoors, draw the curtains and turn off lights, TV, radio, phone, and block out any other distractions to the best of your ability.

You may choose to play relaxing music or a tape/CD that features rhythmic drumming or chanting (without words). If you prefer, you can drum and/or chant yourself. The purpose is to relax and put yourself into a light trance state where your consciousness is free to soar beyond the limits of our ordinary, physical realm.

Sit or lie down in a comfortable place (but don't get so comfortable that you fall asleep). Close your eyes and breathe slowly and deeply, concentrating on your breathing. Picture or mentally call to your spirit animal helper. Then ask your spirit animal helper to be your guide as you travel into your future. It's usually best to specify your reason for traveling ahead in time, for instance, to see what job is right for you or to meet a special person as Joan did in the story above.

Your spirit animal will take you to the place where you will find your answer. With your mind's eye, look about and take note of the people, scenery, and activities going on around you. What you experience may be like watching a movie, or you may be part of the action. It is best to participate if you can.

You may feel your eyelids flutter involuntarily and your body might even twitch a bit. Ignore this. Trust that your spirit animal will guide you safely and show you what you want to see, and help you if need be.

Whenever you're ready, you can reverse the process and return to your ordinary, present-day, waking consciousness. Be sure to thank your spirit animal for its help and tell it you will visit again soon. You'll "awaken" refreshed and full of new insight. While the experience is still clear in your mind, write down the important details so you can refer to them later.

If nothing much happens the first time you take this spirit journey, don't be discouraged. It may take several attempts before you succeed, especially if you aren't accustomed to meditation and creative visualization. Be patient and keep trying. As with everything, practice makes perfect. Know that it will happen. Your spirit animal wants to journey with you as much as you want to be with it.

PART TWO

SPIRIT ANIMALS

SPECIAL POWERS

AND THEIR

CHAPTER FOUR

How To Use Part Two

In Part Two, we'll get acquainted with thirty spirit animal helpers and the physical animals who are their counterparts in the earthly realm. By now you've probably identified your primary spirit animal and established a connection with it. Once you've developed a relationship with your principal animal guide, s/he will introduce you to other animals who can help you.

CALLING ON SPIRIT ANIMALS IN SPECIAL SITUATIONS

Each animal has special qualities and attributes that can help you in specific situations. They will gladly lend their powers to you when you need them. Sometimes these animals appear to you of their own accord–in a dream, a vision, or in the form of a physical animal–to bring you a message or to alert you to something. Other times they may wait until you request their assistance. As you read Chapter Five, you'll learn which matters each animals is most capable of handling.

Choosing the Right Animal to Help You

If you are confronted with a special problem or circumstance and need the help of one or more spirit animals, begin by reading Chapter Five. Most likely, one of the birds, animals, reptiles, or insects discussed there will be able to assist you.

It can also be beneficial to study various animals' habits and habitats to see if there are any similarities to your own situation. Does the animal live in an urban environment or in the wild? Does it interact with people or not? Is it nocturnal or diurnal? Does it migrate or hibernate in winter? For example, if your present concern involves associating with other people, read about animals who live in herds or flocks to see how they handle their relationships.

You might also want to think back over your past to see if you have confronted similar challenges or opportunities before. Our lives are cyclic, so similar situations tend to recur in cycles. For instance, every year at the same time, every seven years, or every twelve years. Michael has noticed that he usually starts new jobs in the spring.

Beverly always has an urge to travel in the fall. As you recall your own cycles, notice whether a particular animal was prominent in your life at those times–this animal could help you now.

Borrowing a Spirit Animal's Power

Once you have determined which animal(s) to call on for assistance, you may want to perform a ritual as a way of invoking the animal's power. Rituals are systematic practices done to heighten feeling, awareness, and intention. They enable us to connect with the consciousness of the universe and to feel at one with all things. Rituals may be simple or complex, short or lengthy, private or done with a group—whatever works best for you.

RITUALS FOR SPECIAL SITUATIONS

Before you begin your ritual, it's a good idea to learn as much as possible about the animal you wish to petition. You could read a book or watch a nature show about it on TV. If the animal is native to your area, you might want to observe it in its natural habitat. Or, you could visit a zoo or wildlife center to study the animal's movements and behavior.

It's also important to be very clear in your own mind about what your purpose is. You might even wish to write down your intention on a piece of paper and keep it present during your ritual.

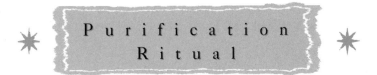

P u r i f i c a t i o n
R i t u a l

This ritual can be done by itself or as a prelude to any of the following rituals. Its purpose is to create a magical space to meet with your spirit animal. Make sure to collect all the tools you need for this ritual before you begin. Gather together the following items:

- a white candle
- a bundle of sage
- matches
- a small drum or rattle
- a jar or dish of water
- cornmeal

* Go to a place where you won't be disturbed for at least half an hour. It can be a room in your own home or a peaceful spot outdoors.

* Begin by emptying your mind of all negative thoughts. You may want to play relaxing music, meditate or do some breathing exercises (see Chapter Two) to help calm your mind and body.

* Holding the jar or dish of water, face east and begin walking in a clockwise circle around your room or space. Sprinkle a few drops of water along your path as you go.

⁎ Next, light the bundle of sage and carry it with you as you walk around the circle once more, trailing its smoke behind you.

⁎ Now, walk to each of the four directions–east, south, west, and north–and sprinkle a pinch of cornmeal in each corner. Say a prayer to your spirit animal at each spot asking it to join you now.

⁎ Sit in the center of the circle and light your candle. Place it on the ground or floor in front of you.

⁎ Begin beating your drum or shaking your rattle in a rhythmic manner.

⁎ Close your eyes and think about your spirit animal. Call its name mentally or aloud. When you feel its presence near you, ask it to lend you its power to help you achieve your intention.

⁎ Sit and commune with your spirit animal helper as long as you wish.

⁎ When you're ready to leave, sprinkle water on the candle's flame, pinch it out with your fingers or use a candle snuffer to put it out. Don't blow it out.

⁎ Thank your spirit animal for its assistance.

⁎ Retrace the circle, but this time walk in a counterclockwise direction.

* Collect your magical tools and store them until you want to perform this ritual again.

Art Ritual

Many Native American tribes and other indigenous people throughout the world have created visual representations of spirit animals to attract the animals' help. We see examples of this in cave paintings, figurines and statues, wood carvings, hand-decorated clothing, musical instruments, jewelry, and pottery. The Oglala, for instance, often did exquisite beadwork on ceremonial garments and decorated their shields with sacred "medicine paintings." Some tribes use different colored sand to create marvelous paintings on the ground.

You don't have to be Rembrandt to perform this very effective art ritual. Choose the art form with which you feel most comfortable: painting, sewing, carving, et cetera.

* Begin by finding a quiet place and clearing your mind of all negative thoughts. You may want to play relaxing music, or do some breathing or meditation exercises to help quiet and center yourself.

* Ask your spirit animal helper to guide your hands and your eyes as you create your work of art.

* Using the medium you have chosen, depict the spirit animal you are seeking to attract. Don't judge yourself or your efforts—simply draw, stitch, carve, or form the animal as best you can. Your image may be realistic or stylized—it is your choice. Depending on your skill level, you may also want to show the situation, purpose, or intent for which this ritual is being performed.

* As you work, repeatedly state aloud your request or your purpose for calling on this animal for help. Your intent will become entwined with every stroke of the brush or stitch you make.

* While you work, you may experience the animal's presence or feel inspired by qualities associated with the animal. For instance, if you are seeking help from a lion you might feel strong, self-confident, or courageous during your ritual as the animal's energy merges with your own.

* When you have finished, thank your spirit animal for its help.

* Display your work of art in a place where you will see it often. You may wear it or use it, but only for special purposes that are connected with the spirit animal and the purpose for which the item was created. This is a ceremonial piece not a utilitarian one, and should be treated as such.

Drumming Ritual

Shamans in all parts of the world often use drums to produce an altered state of consciousness and to align their own body rhythms with the cosmic pulse of life. You can too. Either purchase a small drum or make your own. If you decide to make your own, you may want to decorate it with pictures of your spirit animal(s).

* Find a quiet place where you won't be disturbed. Calm your mind and eliminate all negative thoughts. Be confident that your ritual will be successful.

* Start striking your drum repeatedly with a slow, rhythmic beat. You might want to play in time to your own heartbeat. Do this for about five minutes, or until you feel attuned to the rhythm of the drum. Continue beating your drum throughout the entire ritual.

* When you feel ready, call upon your spirit animal for help. Keep calling it until you sense its presence near you.

* Now ask the animal for its assistance or guidance. You may do this aloud or mentally. You can even sing the request if you prefer. In your mind's eye, imagine the situation you want to create. For instance, if you are seeking a new job, envision yourself working at a new job with a smile on your face.

⋆ Continue drumming for as long as you like. If you want, you can tie this ritual into the following one. When you feel ready, gradually slow your beating until you finally come to a stop. Now thank your spirit animal for its help.

Dancing
Ritual

Indigenous people in North and South America, Africa, Europe, the South Sea Islands, and Australia all dance to awaken their own energy and to tap into the natural rhythms of the earth. In some ceremonial situations, music and dance can actually produce a trance-like sensation. We have all experienced the power, joy, and excitement that music and dancing inspire in us.

This ritual can begin with the drumming ritual above. Or, you may choose instead to play a tape or CD that has a strong, rhythmic beat that you find inspiring. It's best <u>not</u> to play music that has other associations for you, such as a favorite song from your youth or a popular hit tune. The music you choose for this purpose should be played only during your rituals.

⋆ Find a place where you won't be disturbed. Clear your head of any negative thoughts and let yourself relax.

* Play your music for about five minutes or until you feel inspired by its rhythms. During this time, start moving your body to the beat. Don't worry about performing any special dance steps, just let yourself sway in time with the music.

* Now begin imitating the movements of the animal whose help you desire. Jump, crawl, run, slither, stride, toss your head or flap your arms. Imagine you are becoming one with the animal.

* Sing the animal's song. Roar, chirp, neigh, or bark.

* As you begin to sense the animal's presence, ask it to lend you its power to help you achieve your purpose.

* Continue dancing and mimicking your animal for as long as you wish. When you finish, thank your spirit animal helper for its assistance.

These are only a few rituals you can use to call upon your spirit animal helpers. You can also design your own rituals or modify these to suit your purposes. The important things to remember are to stay focused on your objective, keep a positive attitude, and respect the animal you are petitioning. You may choose to incorporate objects that have special meaning for you, such as crystals, feathers, or gemstones, into your rituals. You may decide to perform a ritual at a certain time of the month or year, such as during the full moon or one of the four seasonal solstices.

You might even want to create a ritual that has special connections with the animal you are asking for help. For instance, if the animal is a water creature such as an otter, dolphin, or swan you might want to do a ritual in a pool, pond, or bathtub. Or, you might want to wear a mask or costume that represents your animal helper. As you learn more about various animals in the next chapter, you'll get ideas that can be included in your rituals and ceremonies.

CHAPTER FIVE

Thirty Spirit Animal Helpers

N ow it's time to meet thirty animals and learn about
their special characteristics and powers. Many of
the traits and attributes we connect with the earthly
members of the animal kingdom can be found in the people
who have these animals as spirit helpers. If you strongly
identify with the traits and attributes of an animal, perhaps
you are aligned in power with this spirit helper. It may be
your primary animal guide.

As we found earlier, certain animals come to us at
certain times in our lives–physically, or in dream images or
other visions. When this happens, the animal usually has a
special message for us. As you read about the following

animals, keep in mind that if you are in the habit of seeing the animal on a regular basis (if you share your home with a cat or dog, for instance), it probably has a different meaning than if you spot an animal in an unusual situation (such as the Boston joggers who encountered a runaway moose in the city's streets). An animal companion with which you have a close connection may be the manifestation of your primary spirit helper, while an animal you come upon unexpectedly or in a vivid dream might be a temporary helper or the bearer of important information.

The more you work with your animal helpers, the more you'll be able to benefit from their wisdom and the more frequently you'll find they assist you in your daily life.

BEAR

Traits and Attributes

➤ Bears are large, strong, and potentially dangerous creatures, but unless provoked they tend to be rather shy. Extremely swift, especially in the woods, they can easily outrun humans and are capable of climbing trees. In the winter while they sleep in their dens, bears live off accumulated fat and their bodily systems slow down measurably. It is during this deep winter's sleep that the mother bear gives birth to her cubs. There are many species of bears including the huge grizzly, the panda, and the most common North American variety, the gentle and playful black bear (which, incidentally, can be brown).

People for whom the bear is a spirit guide and helper can be formidable adversaries

Myths And Folklore About The Animal

or fierce, loyal protectors. Generally patient and peace-loving, it takes a lot to anger them, but you don't want to get on their wrong side! Their slow, quiet nature can cause others to misjudge their true speed and perceptual abilities. They are devoted to their children and loved ones. Bear-people may be more active and happy in the summer months than the winter ones, becoming reclusive as cold weather draws near.

➤ Along with the deer, the bear is the companion of the Roman goddess Diana (called Artemis by the Greeks). The bear is also seen in the northern skies as Ursa Major or "The Great Bear" (the Big Dipper) and Ursa Minor (the Little Dipper). Native Americans believed there was a strong connection between bears and humans because both could walk on two legs. Some consider the bear one of the last wild creatures. However, for nearly a century American children have gone to sleep cuddling Teddy bears.

Strength

Protection

Inner wisdom

If you see a bear, either in its natural habitat or in a dream or other vision, it may be a sign that you must go deep within yourself and draw on your instinctive powers or other natural resources. In some instances, it suggests that you should withdraw from the world to reflect and be alone; at other times it advises you to "come out of your cave" and be more social. The bear also points out that you are someone who can help others, but you may not be using your abilities properly.

Traits You Can Borrow (Acquire) From This Spirit Animal

What it Means if You See This Animal or if it Comes to You

BEAVER

Traits and Attributes

➤ The beaver is best known for its hard-working, industrious nature, thus the expression "busy as a beaver." Methodical and diligent, this architect of the animal world chews through tree trunks and builds a durable, ingenious dam for its home, of which a construction engineer would be proud. This amphibious creature can stay under water for fifteen minutes. It lives in a close family group and mates for life.

People who have this animal as a spirit helper are often strong-willed, determined, resourceful, and industrious–like the beaver itself. Persevering and reliable, they stick with a task until it's finished and usually achieve their objectives no matter how long it takes.

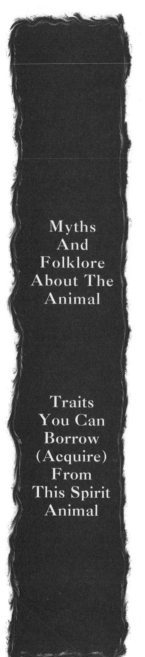

Myths And Folklore About The Animal

Traits You Can Borrow (Acquire) From This Spirit Animal

They aren't satisfied with ideas and dreams; they want to see their visions take physical form. These practical people are concerned with creating security and protection for themselves and their families, and will work hard to provide a stable home. On the negative side, they can be stubborn, overly conservative, and materialistic.

➤ The beaver was a totem for the mystical order of Freemasons, perhaps because of its ability to traverse both the terrestrial and watery worlds, or perhaps because of the many secret tunnels and "doors" or access ways it cleverly constructs in its dam-home.

➤ **Accomplishment**

Practicality

Creativity

If you see a beaver, either in its natural ◄ habitat or in a dream or vision quest, it means you should strive to be more industrious and enterprising. Perhaps it is time to act on your dreams. The beaver tells you that success will come if you are persistent. In order to fulfill your goals, you may need to create a stable base of operation or become more secure and practical in your lifestyle. However, the beaver also warns against being too stubborn or possessive–of people or material goods.

What it Means if You See This Animal or if it Comes to You

BEE

Traits and Attributes

➤ Like the beaver, the bee is known for being industrious and hardworking. We describe a person who is always doing something as being "busy as a bee." In the plant kingdom, the bee is essential to the process of fertilization; without this useful insect, many of the fruits and flowers we enjoy would not exist. The honey it produces is a delicious and much-prized commodity. There is even some evidence to indicate that bee pollen and bee stings may have other healthful properties. Bees live in hierarchical colonies, with a single queen presiding over many drones and workers.

People for whom the bee is a spirit guide and helper are often active, energetic, tireless workers. They pride themselves on their

**Myths
And
Folklore
About The
Animal**

**Traits
You Can
Borrow
(Acquire)
From
This Spirit
Animal**

productivity and their ability to do many things efficiently. Sexuality and fertility are often central to the lives of bee-people, though in some cases their fertility and creativity may take an artistic form. Negatively, these individuals may be so busy and involved in so many activities that they don't take time to notice their surroundings. They need to slow down and "smell the flowers."

➤   The ancient Greeks thought of the bee as the priestess or right-hand-maiden of the goddess Aphrodite. Her role as pollinator made her an important creative power in the garden of life and her honey was considered an elixir for the gods. In ancient Egypt, the bee was a symbol of royalty. The Celts connected bees with wisdom and hidden knowledge.

➤   **Activity**

Industry

Fertility

If you see a bee, either in its natural habitat or in a dream or vision quest, it may be telling you to pay attention to your productivity. Are you producing enough? Do you enjoy your labor and its fruits? Are you so busy you never have time to do what you want? When the bee appears, it may be the start of a fertile time, especially for artistic people. In some instances, it might indicate pregnancy. It can also suggest that you may need to examine your own sexuality or your attitudes toward sex in general.

What it Means if You See This Animal or if it Comes to You

BUTTERFLY

Traits and Attributes

➤ Butterflies are prized for their beauty, delicacy and grace. Like air spirits, they seem to skip or dance as they flit from flower to flower. But despite its fragility, the monarch butterfly makes an incredible annual migration of 2,000 miles. Perhaps the most fascinating characteristic of the butterfly is its ability to transform itself from a caterpillar, which has made it the subject of many myths and legends.

People who have the butterfly as a spirit helper may also demonstrate a joyful, playful, carefree attitude. They love beautiful things and want to experience as much happiness and beauty as possible. As a result, they rarely stick with one thing for long for fear of missing out on something better. Some of them have an

Myths And Folklore About The Animal

other-worldly or ethereal quality. Negatively, they can be fickle, superficial, childish, or unreliable. Butterfly people often go through many changes in their lives, and may completely transform themselves over time.

➤ The Butterfly Maiden is a springtime nature spirit of the Hopi people, and is sometimes fashioned as a *kachina* doll to remind children of the invisible spirits around them. To the Chinese, the butterfly is a symbol of marital happiness. Early Christians saw it as a symbol of the soul. Perhaps no creature is more closely associated with transformation, a theme that can be found in many cultures.

Traits You Can Borrow (Acquire) From This Spirit Animal

➤ **Joy**

Friendliness

Changeability

When you see a butterfly, either in its natural habitat or in a dream or other vision, it may be a signal that change is coming. Or, it may be telling you that you need to make a change in your life or your attitudes, and that it is there to help. Butterflies also appear to us when we need to lighten up, to detach ourselves from our cares and responsibilities, and become more joyful, playful, or sociable.

What it Means if You See This Animal or if it Comes to You

CAT

Traits and Attributes

➤ Known for their grace, cleanliness, and cleverness, cats are now the most popular pet in North America. Intensely curious, their quickness and exceptional eyesight, which allows them to see at night, make them excellent hunters. Their ability to land on their feet when falling from high places may be responsible for the idea that cats have nine lives. Basically nocturnal, cats tend to be loners although they can form friendships with other animals. Cats are the only creatures that purr–a phenomenon that still baffles scientists. Cat-lovers admire the animal's independence and self-possessed dignity but, as anyone who lives with a cat will tell you, they are truly affectionate pets.

Myths And Folklore About The Animal

Traits You Can Borrow (Acquire) From This Spirit Animal

Those who have the cat as a spirit helper are independent and intellectually curious individuals who can't bear to be ordered about. Like the animal, they tend to be fastidious and discriminating about their home, diet, and companions. They value beauty and comfort, and usually possess much grace and poise. Often there is a mysterious quality about them and they don't open up to just anyone. Some cat-people function best at night and like to sleep late. On the negative side, these people may be restless, lazy, unwilling to make commitments, or anti-social.

➤   In ancient Egypt, cats were highly revered and pampered by royalty. Bast, the Egyptian goddess of pleasure, was depicted with a cat companion and sometimes as half-cat, half-woman. The Hindu goddess Shasti is often pictured riding on a cat. In many matriarchal cultures that predated Christianity the cat was considered a divine being.

➤   **Grace**

Independence

Intelligence

Cats are associated with magic and
mystery, so if a cat comes to you or you see a
cat in a dream or other vision, it may mean
you possess magical or mysterious powers but
aren't using them properly. It's also possible
that something magical is about to happen. A
cat might also appear to you when you need
to be more independent or more
discriminating in your choice of companions.

What it
Means
if You
See This
Animal
or if it
Comes
to You

CHEETAH

Traits and Attributes

➤ One of the fastest animals on earth, it only takes the cheetah three seconds to go from standing still to running 70 mph. However, they can only keep up this top speed for a short time. Cheetahs are great hunters and stalk their prey with silent, graceful stealth. They have few enemies and are extremely powerful. Like most big cats, cheetahs are independent creatures although they sometimes hunt together in pairs or small groups.

People who have the cheetah as a spirit helper are strong, assertive individuals who cannot easily be intimidated. Some of them are quick-witted and sharp-tongued, and may insult or hurt others without even realizing it. Once they set a goal for themselves, they go after it full speed ahead. They aren't afraid of

Myths And Folklore About The Animal

Traits You Can Borrow (Acquire) From This Spirit Animal

the potential risks involved and often demonstrate tremendous courage. Consequently, they strive for great heights and are willing to attempt things other people wouldn't consider. They aren't afraid of "long shots" or overwhelming odds. However, cheetah-people tend to be impatient and if they don't accomplish their objectives relatively quickly, may lose interest.

➤ The cheetah is sometimes associated with the Egyptian sun goddess Sekmet, who is often depicted as having the head of a wild cat and a woman's body.

➤ **Speed**

Courage

Independence

Decisiveness

If you see a cheetah on safari, in a zoo, or in a dream or other vision, it may mean you need to be more assertive. This animal encourages you to push aggressively for what you want, to take risks, and to use your power decisively. In order to accomplish your goals you must be strong, courageous, and persistent. Or, you may need to increase your pace. In some cases, the cheetah may be telling you to attack or to defend yourself and to do so quickly.

What it Means if You See This Animal or if it Comes to You

CHIPMUNK

Traits and Attributes

➤ Full of nervous energy, chipmunks always seem to be busy scurrying about from place to place, chattering noisily to themselves as they go. Like squirrels, they are gatherers and hoarders who collect food and anything else that catches their fancy. They carry their bounty in their cheek pouches and store it away in their nests for future use. Unlike their relatives, however, chipmunks live in burrows in the ground and spend much of the winter in a deep sleep.

People who have the chipmunk as a spirit helper tend to be hard-working, determined, and efficient. Security-conscious, they apply themselves to earning and saving money, always keeping something in reserve for a rainy day, and they can

Myths And Folklore About The Animal

Traits You Can Borrow (Acquire) From This Spirit Animal

become quite attached to their possessions. They are usually versatile, intellectually quick, chatty, high-strung, and sociable. Chipmunk-people often have difficulty relaxing and can benefit from getting lots of exercise.

➤   The chipmunk's penchant for hoarding food and other goods has caused some cultures to see this animal as a prosperity symbol. One folktale suggests that if you find a chipmunk's nest, it will contain buried treasure.

➤   **Thrift**

   Efficiency

   Work Ethic

   Prosperity

When you see a chipmunk, in its natural habitat or in a dream or other vision, it may be a signal that it's time to get busy or to work harder. Conversely, it can mean you are working too hard and need to learn to relax. This animal also appears to encourage you to save and protect your resources, financial and otherwise, and to become more thrifty and efficient about using your time, talents, and money. Sometimes the chipmunk can symbolize prosperity or investments coming to fruition.

What it Means if You See This Animal or if it Comes to You

Traits and Attributes

➤   The crow is among the most intelligent and wary of all birds. Crows live in large communal roosts and prefer high perches where they can observe everything that's going on. When danger threatens, they noisily warn everyone in the vicinity and sometimes attempt to chase intruders away. Like other birds of prey, rodents are their principal food source. However, they also eat insects, the eggs of other birds, garbage, carrion, and crops. (If your spirit animal helper is the crow, you can also benefit from learning about the mouse, chipmunk, and other small rodents which represent your "shadow" side; see Chapter Two.)

**Myths
And
Folklore
About The
Animal**

People who have the crow as their spirit animal helper are often intelligent, skeptical, and inquisitive. They like to know everything that's going on around them and are always on the alert for danger. Highly social, these people prefer to do things in a group and desire the approval of their peers. Some crow-people enjoy sharing their knowledge with others and may be gifted teachers, writers, or researchers. Although they may be talkative and outspoken, these people can still be trusted to keep a secret.

➤ Native Americans recognized the crow's intelligence and saw the bird as a teacher. They also valued its social, tribal behavior. Some ancient mystery traditions believed the crow was the guardian of magical secrets. The Norse god Odin (or Wodin) kept two ravens named Munin (memory) and Hugin (thought) as companions. Crows even appear in the Bible, where they brought food to the prophet Elijah during his period of hiding in the wilderness. In *feng shui,* the ancient Chinese art of placement, however, the crow is considered an inauspicious sign.

Crows are often viewed as messengers, which may be why Edgar Allen Poe cast the raven in this role in his famous poem. In Roman mythology, the crow was white until the day it carried bad news to the god Apollo, at which time it turned black.

Communication Skills ◄

Wariness

Intelligence

Magical Knowledge

Traits You Can Borrow (Acquire) From This Spirit Animal

When you see a crow, in its natural ◄ habitat or in a dream or other vision, it may be a signal that you should be more alert and wary. In some cases it can suggest that a betrayal is likely or has already occurred. A crow may appear when you begin a new course of study in order to encourage and guide you. Sometimes Crow is alerting you to the arrival of a letter or message.

What it Means if You See This Animal or if it Comes to You

DEER

Traits and Attributes

➤ There are numerous types of deer throughout the world, but in North America, the white-tailed deer is the most common variety. All deer are known for their grace, swiftness, and beauty. Deer generally live in small herds with a single adult male overseeing a number of females. These lovely creatures are fleet-footed, alert, and sensitive, with keenly developed hearing and sense of smell. Their physical appearance enables them to blend into their surroundings so they become virtually invisible to predators.

People who have the deer as their spirit animal helper are usually quick, high-strung, and graceful. They love beauty and are quite discerning. For the most part they are gentle, compassionate, and congenial people who are

Myths And Folklore About The Animal

Traits You Can Borrow (Acquire) From This Spirit Animal

welcome in any social group or gathering. Flighty and changeable, they rarely stick with one thing for long and tend to jump from place to place, idea to idea. On the negative side they can be moody, easily discouraged, and inconsistent.

➤ Diana, the Roman goddess of the forest and guardian of the wilderness (known as Artemis to the Greeks), is often pictured with a deer as her companion. In some early pagan cultures, a new king was initiated at a ceremony in which he dressed as a stag, wearing the antlers of the male deer. Santa Claus is carried through the heavens in a sleigh drawn by magical flying reindeer, bringing gifts of hope and joy during the darkest time of the year.

➤ **Grace**

Loveliness

Sensitivity

If you see this animal, in its natural ◄
habitat or in a dream or other vision, it may
be telling you that you need more beauty in
your life. The deer also appears when it's
time to cultivate sympathy, gentleness, or
compassion for others. If you have been
working too hard or assuming too much
responsibility, the deer may be urging you to
let others take control for awhile. On the
other hand, seeing a deer can be symbolic of
flightiness and the need to develop self-
discipline, consistency, and concentration.

What it
Means
if You
See This
Animal
or if it
Comes
to You

DOG

➤ Descended from wolves, dogs were one of the first animals to be domesticated and they have lived with people for about 10,000 years. They possess exceptional hearing and a keen sense of smell. Dogs are known for their loyalty and devotion. Sometimes called "man's best friend," these affectionate animals shower their human companions with unconditional love and stick by them no matter what.

People who have the dog as their spirit animal helper are usually good-natured, affectionate, friendly people. They don't like being alone and enjoy the company of others. Optimistic, they try to find the good in everyone and are not judgmental. In relationships, they are loyal and devoted. As

Myths And Folklore About The Animal

Traits You Can Borrow (Acquire) From This Spirit Animal

parents, they are nurturing, protective, and kind. Negatively, dog-people can be indiscriminate and may allow others to take advantage of them. They may also have trouble motivating themselves and look to others for direction.

➤ In ancient Greece, dogs were thought to be the companions of the dead who guarded their spirits as they traveled to the other side. Early Christians also saw dogs as guardians and connected them with the priesthood. The Greek god Ares had a dog as a companion. In ancient Egypt, the god Anubis was depicted with the head of a wild dog or jackal.

➤ Loyalty

Compassion

Affection

Protection

Because dogs are such loyal and loving creatures, if a dog comes to you or you see a dog in a dream or other vision, it may mean you should become more affectionate and faithful. It can also suggest that you need companionship. In some cases, a dog can symbolize a need for protection or urge you to be more protective of yourself and the people/things you love.

Dogs are also noted for their playfulness, so when a dog appears it may be encouraging you to have fun, play, and enjoy life. Since different dogs have different roles and characteristics, pay attention to the breed of dog you see, for this can also be important. For instance, a setter or bloodhound could suggest you should hunt more deeply for something, while a Doberman might be warning you to be on guard.

What it Means if You See This Animal or if it Comes to You

DOLPHIN

Traits and Attributes

➤ Although they live in the ocean, dolphins are mammals. They are capable of swimming 40 mph and can dive as deep as 300 feet, but must come up for air every couple of minutes. These animals are extremely intelligent, sociable, and communicative, and in captivity they form friendships with humans. Their remarkable sonar ability enables them to locate objects by sensing vibrations, so dolphins have been used by the military, scientists, and researchers in underwater tracking missions.

People who have the dolphin as their spirit animal helper are curious, intelligent, and intuitive, often delving deeply into subjects that interest them. Sociable and

Traits
You Can
Borrow
(Acquire)
From
This Spirit
Animal

talkative, they also enjoy sharing their knowledge with others and may have a large circle of friends.

➤ The ancient Greeks saw the dolphin as a messenger of the gods and believed it was unfortunate to kill one. The dolphin was especially sacred to the Greek god Apollo. Early Christians considered it a symbol of salvation. Sailors often report dolphins swimming alongside their boats, so it may be that these graceful and vocal creatures were the source of mariners' tales about mermaids and sirens.

➤ **Intelligence**

Communication Skills

Curiosity

If you see this animal in its natural habitat or in a dream or other vision, it may be telling you to expand your awareness beyond your own family or town and to see yourself as a member of the global community.

Dolphins are teachers, so this animal may be a signal that you are about to learn something, that you need to pay more attention to your intellectual development, or that you have something to communicate to others. Another reason the dolphin may appear to you is to encourage you to enjoy life and become more playful.

What it Means if You See This Animal or if it Comes to You

Traits and Attributes

➤ The most common waterfowl in North America, ducks are capable of traveling on foot (earth), swimming (water), and flying (air), so they are comfortable almost anyplace. Consequently, they are often believed to symbolize balance. Both wild and domesticated ducks are gregarious creatures who live in flocks and are rarely found alone. Domesticated ducks will waddle along behind their human keepers, following them everywhere they go. Many northern ducks migrate to warm regions during the winter months and may change their plumage twice a year.

People who have the duck as a spirit animal helper are adaptable and able to make

Myths And Folklore About The Animal

Traits You Can Borrow (Acquire) From This Spirit Animal

the best of whatever situation they find themselves in. Like their totem animal, they may prefer warm climates and head south each year at the first sign of winter. These friendly, sociable individuals generally go along with the crowd and tend to be "creatures of habit." Water, the duck's principal element, is a common symbol for the emotions, so duck-people usually feel comfortable in emotional relationships.

➤   In an Iroquois tale, ducks are said to have propelled the boats of mythological heroes and devils. Ducks were also seen as guides who, because they can travel by land, water, or air, were able to lead a hero to his destination wherever it might be.

➤   **Balance**

Emotional Comfort

Adaptability

Wild Duck: Adventurousness

If you see this animal, in its natural  habitat or in a dream or other vision, it may be an indication that you need to establish balance in your life or learn to be more adaptable. The duck also appears to you to advise you to pay more attention to your emotions and your close personal relationships.

What it Means if You See This Animal or if it Comes to You

ELEPHANT

Traits and Attributes

➤ The largest mammal on earth, elephants are native only to Africa and southern Asia. Their great size and tremendous strength are their most notable features, but elephants are also known for being intelligent and emotional, often displaying strong feelings toward other members of their herd. Elephants have poor eyesight, but use their long, versatile trunks and keen sense of smell to guide them. Their ivory tusks are used for defensive purposes as well as for digging food. Except at mating time, elephants usually live separate lives primarily according to sex: females and calves generally live together, guided by an older cow, while males stay together in "bachelor" groups.

Myths And Folklore About The Animal

People who have the elephant as a spirit animal helper may possess great physical, sexual, and/or emotional power. They are usually intelligent and may be interested in ancient wisdom, the past, and upholding the traditions of family and society. Demonstratively affectionate toward their friends and relatives, these people tend to hold grudges and never forget an injury or slight. Extremely loyal themselves, if they feel they have been treated badly or betrayed, they may seek revenge.

➤ In Hindu mythology, the god Ganesh is portrayed with the head of an elephant. Ganesh is believed to help human beings overcome obstacles and hardships in their lives. In some parts of southern Asia, elephants are associated with fertility and male elephants are viewed as symbols of sexual power. Royalty rode on elephants and soldiers used them to overpower their foes in battle. The god Indra is often viewed with elephant companions. Some cultures consider the elephant as the most sacred of all animals, and the Buddha's mother, while she was pregnant, is said to have dreamed that she carried a white elephant in her womb.

Intelligence ◄

Strength

Loyalty

If you see this animal, in its natural ◄
habitat or in a dream or other vision, it may
suggest that you have a good mind, but need
to develop or use it more. Perhaps it's time to
concentrate on mental things rather than
physical ones. Sometimes it symbolizes
ancient wisdom and uncovering fundamental
truths. The elephant may also appear to urge
you to help those who are less powerful or to
encourage you to press on in order to
overcome difficulties.

Traits
You Can
Borrow
(Acquire)
From
This Spirit
Animal

What it
Means
if You
See This
Animal
or if it
Comes
to You

FOX

Traits and Attributes

➤ These agile, graceful members of the canine family are known for their cunning and stealth. Their long, soft fur is either gray, reddish-brown, or white, depending on their habitat, and not only provides protection from heat and cold, but also enables them to blend into their surroundings. They tend to be nocturnal loners, preying on small rodents for food. Unlike dogs, foxes don't pant but release excess body heat through their large, sensitive ears.

People who have the fox as their spirit helper are able to use their cleverness and cunning to delight and manipulate others. Intuitive and perceptive, they are keen observers of other people's behavior. Sometimes they can be tricksters who are not

Traits
You Can
Borrow
(Acquire)
From
This Spirit
Animal

what they seem and may have hidden motives. Fox-people are so charming and graceful that they can cause others to overlook their faults.

➤   In some Native American tribes, the fox is seen as possessing feminine traits. The Cherokee believed Fox knew the cure for frostbite and the Apaches revered it for bringing fire to humankind. In some cultures, the animal's ability to blend into its environment has earned it an association with shapeshifting, magic, and invisibility. Chinese folklore suggests that the fox is capable of taking on a human form, usually as a beautiful "foxy" young woman. The ancient Persians saw it as a sacred animal who assisted the dead in crossing over into heaven. The fable *The Fox and the Grapes* depicts this animal as being both clever and spiteful.

➤   **Ingenuity**

Cunning

Keen Powers Of Observation

Unobtrusiveness

If you see a fox, in its natural habitat ◄ or in a dream or other vision, it may suggest that you need to leave your naiveté and innocence behind. It's time to become more wily. The fox might also appear to warn you that someone is watching you or that you should observe and keep silent. In some instances, the fox may point out to you that are you becoming a recluse, disappearing into the background. On the other hand, you may be too visible and could benefit from keeping a low profile for a while.

What it Means if You See This Animal or if it Comes to You

125

GIRAFFE

Traits and Attributes

➤   The most notable characteristic of this peculiar-looking animal is its exceptionally long neck. The tallest of all animals, the giraffe stands up to eighteen feet high and its great height enables it to see far into the distance. With its long legs, the giraffe can run up to 30 mph. Giraffes are sociable creatures who develop bonds with others in their herd and family.

    People who have the giraffe as their spirit helper often have keen vision and intuition, and are able to see things other people miss. Because of their ability to see the big picture, these individuals tend to be easy-going and don't let everyday pressures get to them. However, like the giraffe, they may have their heads in the sky and not be

Myths
And
Folklore
About The
Animal

Traits
You Can
Borrow
(Acquire)
From
This Spirit
Animal

well grounded in the physical world. They are usually friendly, talkative people who may be capable of psychic communication.

➤   Many African tribes see the giraffe as a symbol of friendship. The lump between the giraffe's two horns is sometimes thought to be a "third eye," signifying psychic ability.

➤   **A Broader Perspective on Life**

Intuition

If you see a giraffe, in its natural habitat or in a dream or other vision, it may be reminding you to look at the big picture rather than the details. This animal encourages you to look ahead to your future. It also appears when you need to pay attention to how you are communicating with others.

What it Means if You See This Animal or if it Comes to You

GOAT

Traits and Attributes

➤ Both wild mountain goats and their domesticated relatives are hardy creatures, known for their ability to survive in terrain where other animals would perish. Sure-footed mountain goats scale craggy peaks with astounding grace; domestic goats thrive in marginal regions where the vegetation is too poor for cattle and other livestock.

People who have the goat as their spirit helper are often rugged, hard-working, no-nonsense individuals. Once they make up their minds they are not easily deterred from their goals and can be a bit stubborn. They understand the importance of striving to reach new heights. Self-reliant, goat-people are confident that they will always land on their feet. Though they may be frugal and

Myths And Folklore About The Animal

Traits You Can Borrow (Acquire) From This Spirit Animal

live quite modestly, they enjoy creature comforts and physical pleasures.

➤ The most familiar goat deity is Pan, the pipe-playing Roman nature god with a man's torso and a goat's horns, hind legs, and feet. A playful, merry being and a wonderful musician, he was the god of shepherds and goatherds. The goat is also the symbol for the astrological sign Capricorn. As such, it signifies persistence and overcoming adversity through determination.

➤ **Ambition**

Perseverance

Appreciation of Nature And Earthly Delights

If you see a goat, in its natural habitat ◄ or in a dream or other vision, it may be telling you to get serious about a goal or project, or to apply more effort so you can accomplish your objective. In some instances, this animal may appear when you have been working too hard to encourage you to lighten up. The goat could also be a signal that a new endeavor is about to enter your life and that you should pursue it slowly, industriously, and carefully.

What it Means if You See This Animal or if it Comes to You

GOOSE

Traits and Attributes

➤ These large, high-flying waterfowl are relatives of the duck and the swan. Wild geese, including the Canadian and snow geese, live in marshy areas, along streams, rivers, and lakes. Sociable creatures, they live in large flocks, mate for life, and migrate together annually flying in a distinctive "V" formation. Domesticated geese often serve as "watchdogs," honking noisily and hissing at strangers.

People who have the goose as their spirit helper tend to be perfectionists and may become irritable when things don't go their way. Ambitious, they want to soar to great heights and always keep their eyes focused on the distant horizon. Like the goose, who can

**Myths
And
Folklore
About The
Animal**

**Traits
You Can
Borrow
(Acquire)
From
This Spirit
Animal**

fly, swim, and walk on dry land, they are versatile individuals, capable of achieving success in many areas. Goose-people possess keen imaginations and acute vision, and are always ready to venture into new frontiers. They are generally devoted partners and parents, and value the companionship and approval of their peers.

➤ To the early Celts, the goose was a favorite totem and was considered a symbol of purification and renewal. The goose appears in many European fairy tales and stories including *Mother Goose* and *The Goose That Laid The Golden Egg*. Some Native American tribes see the wild goose as a symbol of the Great Dreamer who inspires them to greatness.

➤ **Wild Goose:**
 Fidelity
 Perfectionism
 Adventurousness

Domestic goose:
 Protectiveness
 Versatility

If you see a goose, in its natural habitat or in a dream or other vision, it may be an indication that you should venture further afield and set your sights higher. It encourages you to draw on your inner strength and to be true to yourself. The goose may also suggest you need to protect yourself, your resources, or your loved ones. In some instances, the goose appears when a trip is imminent.

What it Means if You See This Animal or if it Comes to You

Traits and Attributes

➤ Perhaps no animal has been more important and more admired in our culture than the horse. Horses were first used for transportation by the Sumerians nearly 5,000 years ago. They were reintroduced into North America by the Spaniards in the 16th century, where they were used for riding, pulling carriages and wagons, cultivating fields, and many other tasks. Horses were vital to the development of many countries throughout the world and at the turn of this century, there were about 20 million domestic horses in North America. Herds of wild horses, or mustangs, still roam parts of this continent. The horse has long been valued for its strength, speed, and beauty. In dreams, it is considered to represent freedom, basic instincts, and personal power.

Myths And Folklore About The Animal

People who have the horse as their spirit helper are often restless, energetic, free-spirited individuals who love to travel. They have an adventurous nature and can be quite temperamental, especially when constrained. They don't like taking orders and can be hard-headed and rebellious. Often they are powerful, charismatic, sexually attractive people who can inspire others and pull them along in their wake.

➤ Pegasus was the winged horse of the Greek muses and the mount of Poseidon's son Bellerophon. He now resides in the heavens as a constellation of stars. In Greek mythology, the sun god Apollo travels across the sky in a chariot pulled by galloping stallions. Surya, the Hindu sun god, also rides in a horse-drawn chariot. The Norse god Odin (Wodin) is often depicted as riding a horse with eight legs. In Western astrology, the sign Sagittarius is symbolized by the centaur who has a man's torso and the body of a horse. The horse is also one of the twelve animals in Chinese astrology.

Racehorse:	Speed
	Grace
Mustang:	Freedom
	Adventurousness
Workhorse:	Determination
	Strength
	Achievement
Stallion:	Sexual Energy
	Vitality

Traits You Can Borrow (Acquire) From This Spirit Animal

If a horse comes to you or you see one in a dream or other vision, it may be a sign that your independence is being restrained. Perhaps you need to take more risks and embrace freedom. In some cases, the horse appears when you are about to take a trip; or it might encourage you to embark on a new journey, physically or mentally. The horse may also be suggesting that you aren't expressing your sexuality adequately.

What it Means if You See This Animal or if it Comes to You

Pay attention to your position in relation to the horse. Riding on the horse's back shows that you are master of your personal power and are engaging it fully. Watching a horse run may mean you are standing on the sidelines rather than participating in the action. A stampeding horse can suggest that your emotions are out of control. A horse pulling a heavy load might indicate that your freedom is being limited by your responsibilities.

LADYBUG

Traits and Attributes

➤ Most ladybugs are red or yellow with dark spots, though some are solid colored. Like many insects, ladybugs go through a complete metamorphosis, changing from an egg to a grub to a winged creature during their life cycle. Common to nearly every locale, ladybugs prefer sunshine and warm temperatures and are most active in the summer months, remaining virtually immobile during cold weather.

People who have the ladybug as their spirit helper are practical, nurturing, protective individuals who take good care of their homes and children. Like the insect itself, they may be sun worshippers who are happiest in warm climates or during the summertime when they can be outside

Myths And Folklore About The Animal

enjoying nature or working in the garden. These people are likely to experience many changes or transformations during their lifetimes. Some ladybug-people are interested in hidden knowledge, magic, and spirituality, and may be inclined toward soul-searching.

➤ These small, circular flying beetles are favorites of children. Every child knows that if a ladybug lands near or on you, it is considered good luck to gently place this tiny creature on the top of your hand, make a wish, and when it flies away, your wish will come true. The Ancient Egyptians considered beetles or scarabs to be symbols of the soul, and fashioned jewelry, statues, and other ornaments in their image. They were also seen as messengers of the sun gods. To some Native Americans they represent hidden knowledge and wisdom. Because ladybugs metamorphose from grubs to flying beetles, they have been viewed as symbols of transformation, reincarnation, and new life by many cultures.

Ability to Accept Change ◄

Cleanliness

Healing

Wisdom

If you see a ladybug, in its natural ◄ habitat or in a dream or other vision, it may be a signal that change is coming, or that one phase of your life is ending and another is about to begin. It can also suggest that you need to change something, in particular, you may need to get rid of the "pests" in your life. A ladybug may also appear to you to urge you to let in more sunshine or warmth.

Traits You Can Borrow (Acquire) From This Spirit Animal

What it Means if You See This Animal or if it Comes to You

145

MOUSE

Traits and Attributes

➤ There are dozens of types of mice and they are found virtually everywhere in the world. Mice are known for hoarding food in their nests which they build in underground burrows, trees, birds' nests, as well as human dwellings. The prey of many animals and birds, mice survive by being quiet, attentive, quick, adaptable, and unobtrusive. They are also extremely prolific and have three or four litters each year. It can be helpful to learn about their predators in order to better understand the mouse as a spirit animal.

People who have the mouse as their spirit helper are often rather shy, nervous, and sensitive. They like to curl up in a comfortable chair at home, away from the stress of the outer world. Mouse-people

Myths And Folklore About The Animal

Traits You Can Borrow (Acquire) From This Spirit Animal

abhor any kind of change or upset in their routine. Meticulous and conscientious workers, they are clever when it comes to finding solutions to problems. Like the rodent, they tend to hoard their possessions and may fear poverty.

➤   In the *Iliad,* Apollo is referred to as the mouse-god. One of the twelve signs in Chinese astrology is the rat, a close relative of the mouse. Mice turn up in many fables and stories, such as the tale of the *Three Blind Mice,* but perhaps the most famous mouse of all is Walt Disney's cartoon character Mickey, a modern-day symbol of every man.

➤   **Attention to Detail**

Cleverness

Silent Watchfulness

Humility

If you see a mouse, in its natural habitat or in a dream or other vision, it may suggest that if you remain quiet and unobtrusive, you'll see things you've missed before. A mouse might also appear in order to urge you to pay attention to details. Or, it may tell you that you're scattering your energy by trying to do too many things.

What it Means if You See This Animal or if it Comes to You

Traits and Attributes

➤ A member of the weasel family, the river otter makes its home in a river bank and protects it by placing the entrance under water; the sea otter lives along the rocky shores of the ocean. Extremely curious, the otter is a playful and sociable creature who is equally at home on land or in the water. Its webbed feet and strong tail enable it to swim swiftly and perform water aerobics with great agility. Its diet consists mostly of fish and crustaceans, and it eats and sleeps while floating on its back in the water.

People who have the otter as their spirit helper are outgoing, playful, and are devoted to their families. Some of them have a hard time letting their children go their own way. These individuals are usually well-

Myths And Folklore About The Animal

Traits You Can Borrow (Acquire) From This Spirit Animal

organized, neat, and constructive, and are often skillful managers who know how to adapt to changing circumstances. Like the animal, they are insatiably curious and usually love the water. Although they are always willing to help others, they insist on being independent and resent having restrictions placed on them.

➤   Because it lives in the water, some Native American tribes connected the otter with cleansing and purification.

➤   **Playfulness**

Curiosity

Orderliness

If you see an otter, in its natural habitat or in a dream or other vision, it may be telling you that you need to have more fun and let your worries roll off your back. The otter appears when it's time to renew your sense of wonder and joy at the world around you, and to open yourself up to new experiences.

What it Means if You See This Animal or if it Comes to You

Traits and Attributes

➤   There are many species of owls in North America; all have large, sensitive eyes and keen hearing that enable them to fly and hunt at night. Their nocturnal nature makes them seem mysterious to humans. Generally solitary, owls live alone or with a mate, roosting in high places: trees, the rafters of buildings, towers or steeples. Owls are caring and protective toward their young; while the female sits on her eggs, the male brings her food. When these birds hunt, they demonstrate the same deadly accuracy as falcons and hawks. The owl's primary prey is mice and other small rodents, so it can be helpful to learn about these animals in order to understand your "shadow" side.

Myths And Folklore About The Animal

People who have the owl as their spirit helper are often intrigued by hidden knowledge, mysteries, and secrets. Usually they are quite intuitive and may "know" things before these become obvious to others. Some owl-people are loners who prefer reading and studying to socializing, and many are at their best during the nighttime. Often they are brave, independent adventurers, pioneers and visionaries who need freedom to pursue their life quests in their own way. In the extreme, they can be aggressive risk-takers who reject the company and help of other people.

➤ Myths and stories abound about the owl. The ancient Greeks connected this bird with Athena, the goddess of wisdom. The Gnostics associated the owl with Adam's first wife, Lilith. In pre-Christian Europe, owls were symbols of ancient wisdom and considered sacred. Some ancient cultures linked them with death and reincarnation. Old tombstones are often inscribed with a "death-head" which is sometimes the image of an owl's face and wings. Because of its round, light-colored face and nocturnal habits, the owl has also been connected with the moon. Some Native

American tribes believed the owl possessed healing powers; others viewed Owl as a protector. The Welsh associate owls with fertility.

Clairvoyance ◄

Wisdom

Precision

Traits You Can Borrow (Acquire) From This Spirit Animal

If you see an owl, in its natural ◄ habitat or in a dream or other vision, it may be urging you to develop and use your psychic powers. In some instances, this bird suggests that you should examine someone or something more deeply, or that you should take a closer look at details. It also may advise you to search for secrets or hidden information. Sometimes Owl appears as a prophetic messenger to notify you that something important is about to happen.

What it Means if You See This Animal or if it Comes to You

RABBIT

Traits and Attributes

➤   Rabbits are known for being prolific procreators, giving birth to several litters a year. Young rabbits mature rapidly and are able to survive on their own after only twenty-eight days, a cycle which links the rabbit with the moon. Fleet of foot, with highly developed hearing and sense of smell, rabbits use quickness and defensive action rather than strength and assertiveness to outwit their many predators. Rabbits are most active at dawn and dusk. These are the "in-between" times that the Celts connect with the faery realm which exists between the physical and spirit worlds.

People who have the rabbit as their spirit helper may be agile and speedy, both physically and mentally. They have a

Myths And Folklore About The Animal

tendency to jump from one interest to another, without committing to anything for very long. Some of them are quite affectionate and sensual; most love children. Often they are sensitive, gentle, observant individuals who are alert to everything going on around them. Rabbit-people rarely assert themselves and will usually run away from conflicts.

➤ The ancient Greeks associated the rabbit with Hecate, goddess of the dark moon and guardian of the crossroads. The rabbit is one of the twelve signs in Chinese astrology. Oglala braves decked themselves with rabbit skins in rituals to increase their humility. Because rabbits reproduce rapidly, they are frequently associated with fertility; they appear at Easter as a symbol of birth and rebirth. The fable of *The Hare And The Tortoise* advises us that speed without consistency won't accomplish our aims. In *Alice's Adventures in Wonderland,* the White Rabbit is a magical creature who reveals a strange, new world to Alice.

Gentleness

Versatility

Quickness

Creativity

Traits
You Can
Borrow
(Acquire)
From
This Spirit
Animal

If you see a rabbit, in its natural habitat or in a dream or other vision, it may be suggesting that you need to slow down–especially if you've been hopping about busily from one thing to another. A rabbit may come to encourage you to be gentle, compassionate, and modest in your dealings with others. It can also signify the beginning of a project that will take twenty-eight days to complete or that you are about to enter a twenty-eight day cycle.

What it
Means
if You
See This
Animal
or if it
Comes
to You

RACCOON

Traits and Attributes

➤ Raccoons are renowned for their cleverness, curiosity, and adaptability. Generally they are friendly, sociable animals. With their dexterous paws, they can open just about anything—from doors to garbage cans. This deftness, along with its dark facial "bandit" mask and nocturnal nature, have earned the raccoon a reputation as a bandit. Although they'll eat just about anything, their favorite foods are vegetables and fruit, which they like to "wash" in water before eating it—a behavior that makes us think of them as fastidious. Raccoons prefer to be in wooded areas and often make their nests in trees or hollow logs, though they have also been known to thrive in urban environments.

People who have the raccoon as their spirit helper are often skillful and clever. Intensely curious and resourceful, they able to figure out a solution to any problem. They may also possess a great physical or manual dexterity. Many of them are meticulous, tidy, and efficient in all they do, but run the risk of being overly fussy. Raccoon-people are adaptable and easily adjust to changing situations. Sometimes friendly, sometimes reclusive, these individuals are usually slow to anger but can be ferocious when pushed too far. Negatively, they can be deceptive, sly, and secretive about themselves, while being extremely inquisitive regarding other people's affairs.

➤ Some ancient and aboriginal cultures connected the raccoon with mystery and secrets because it "hides" behind a mask.

Myths And Folklore About The Animal

Traits You Can Borrow (Acquire) From This Spirit Animal

➤ **Cleverness**

Enterprise

Neatness

If you see a raccoon, in its natural habitat or in a dream or other vision, it may be urging you to get organized. It can also mean that you should become more adaptable and act cleverly. In some instances, a raccoon may come to advise you to be more secretive or to mask your objectives; or, it could suggest that you are being devious or deceptive. Raccoon might also be telling you that someone you know is hiding behind a disguise.

What it Means if You See This Animal or if it Comes to You

ROBIN

Traits and Attributes

➤ The robin is a harbinger of spring, one of the first birds to return to northern regions after the cold weather has ended. In years when food is plentiful and conditions are not too severe, this hearty bird may not migrate. One of the most common songbirds in North America, its most notable characteristic is its russet-red breast. The robin's eggs, too, are distinctively colored: a bright sky blue. Female robins may lay three sets of eggs each year, and both parents take care of the young. Male robins compete for territory, using their songs as "weapons."

People who have the robin as their spirit helper tend to be quite vocal and express their opinions strongly. They usually

Myths
And
Folklore
About The
Animal

Traits
You Can
Borrow
(Acquire)
From
This Spirit
Animal

enjoy music, especially singing, and may have powerful, melodious voices. Sometimes they are the most inspiring or colorful orators. Adventurous, hearty individuals, they're not easily intimidated and stand up to their adversaries—especially when their territory is threatened. Often the first to try something new, robin-people can be trendsetters or pioneers. Negatively, they may be argumentative, combative, and boisterous.

➤ An old superstition holds that it's bad luck to steal a robin's egg from the nest and misfortune will befall anyone who does. Another superstition advises making a wish when you see the first robin of spring. The expression "the early bird gets the worm" is believed to refer to the robin, one usually of the earliest birds to be seen in springtime— often with a worm in its beak.

➤ **Daring**

Communication Skills

Musical Appreciation

If you see a robin, in its natural habitat or in a dream or other vision, it suggests that something new is about to enter your life. The robin comes to help you grow through this new experience. A robin's egg can symbolize creativity or signal that a new part of you is about to be born.

What it Means if You See This Animal or if it Comes to You

SALMON

Traits and Attributes

➤ This large and colorful fish is born in fresh water, but soon travels to the sea where it lives for about three to five years until it matures. To spawn, it returns to the exact stream or river where it was born—though scientists are still not sure exactly how it accomplishes this feat—navigating rapids and waterfalls and other obstacles to reach its destination. Both fresh and saltwater varieties of salmon are found in cold water, and it is a popular fish for both food and sport in North America, Russia, Japan, and Northern Europe.

People who have the salmon as their spirit helper are not afraid to confront challenges and rarely take the easy way out. They are proud, passionate, and energetic individuals, who exude confidence and are

often unwilling to compromise their ideas or principles. Many salmon-people are ardent travelers; those who don't physically wander the globe are usually interested in foreign places and cultures. However, they also have a strong attachment to their home and heritage, and even though they may journey far and wide, they try to return to the place of their birth as often as possible.

Myths And Folklore About The Animal

➤ In northern Europe and Britain, the salmon was known as the king of the fishes. To some Native American tribes, the salmon represented longevity. Legend has it that the salmon possesses clairvoyance and magical wisdom because it somehow manages to find its way back to the exact spot of its birth. Like all fish, its element is water, which symbolizes the emotions. Although the salmon's bright pink flesh is most likely the result of its ocean diet, according to superstition, its color is said to be caused by its passionate emotional nature.

Courage ◄

Versatility

Intuition

Traits You Can Borrow (Acquire) From This Spirit Animal

If you see a salmon, in its natural ◄ habitat or in a dream or other vision, it may be a signal that you should expand your horizons. A salmon sometimes appears just before you take a trip. In some instances, you could see a salmon when you are confronting obstacles; it urges you to be more aggressive about overcoming them.

What it Means if You See This Animal or if it Comes to You

SKUNK

Traits and Attributes

➤ The skunk's most distinctive characteristic is its pungent odor which it sprays when it feels threatened or annoyed. Even newborn skunks can spray to repel an adversary. As a result, these small, slow-moving, and gentle animals have few enemies—only great horned owls prey on them. Solitary and nocturnal, skunks are quite adaptable; they'll eat almost anything and can live in either the country or city. The two most common varieties have black fur with broad white stripes, or are black-and-white spotted. Skunks can be found throughout North and Central America.

People who have the skunk as their spirit helper are generally quiet, easy-going, unassuming people, but they naturally

Myths And Folklore About The Animal

Traits You Can Borrow (Acquire) From This Spirit Animal

command respect and fear no one. Because they are secure in their self-esteem, they don't take offense easily at slights or insults. Although they are often loners who prefer a calm, reclusive life, they are adaptable and resourceful, and will do what's necessary to get along. Many skunk-people are quite sensual and attractive; however, they tend to be modest and don't feel a need to boast or put on airs to win attention.

➤   Dakota chiefs tied skunk pelts to their feet to show that they never ran away from danger. The white stripe that runs the length of skunk's body is sometimes thought to represent the *kundalini* energy (or life force) in Eastern traditions. In some cultures, its powerful scent is connected with sexuality and the ability to simultaneously attract and repel.

➤   **Self-esteem**

Adaptability

Strong defenses

If you see a skunk, in its natural habitat or in a dream or other vision, it may be a sign that you should fortify your defenses and protect yourself. Skunk comes to help you strengthen your self-esteem so you can't be easily intimidated or controlled by others.

What it Means if You See This Animal or if it Comes to You

TURTLE

Traits and Attributes

➤ Turtles are the oldest of all the vertebrates and one of the most ancient reptiles. Turtles and tortoises have lots of similarities; the main distinction between them is that turtles live in water, tortoises on land. Many varieties of turtles and tortoises can be found around the world, but all of them possess a most unique feature: a sturdy shell, which serves as their home and affords them protection from virtually all predators. A turtle's metabolism is very slow and it moves as if it has plenty of time–and perhaps it does, since this creature's life span is equal to a human's.

People who have the turtle as their spirit helper are well equipped to protect themselves and to provide shelter for themselves and their

Myths And Folklore About The Animal

Traits You Can Borrow (Acquire) From This Spirit Animal

families. Their survival skills are exceptional. Turtle-people are grounded and determined; they take their time and don't let the hectic pace of the outside world rush them. As a result, they usually accomplish whatever they set out to do.

➤ Many Native Americans see the Earth as a turtle who supports human beings on her back. The Plains Indians also consider the turtle to be a wise, old woman with many powers, among them the ability to heal women's diseases. In some Eastern cultures, the shell of the turtle is a symbol of heaven. Nigerians associate the turtle with the female sex organs.

➤ **Wisdom**

Longevity

Patience

Perseverance

If you see a turtle, in its natural habitat or in a dream or other vision, it may be a sign that your life is becoming too frenetic and you need to slow down. In some cases, it may advise you to pull back into your shell and avoid the hubbub of the world around you for a time. The turtle often appears when you are trying to rush things, and urges you to be patient, to let things unfold in due time.

What it Means if You See This Animal or if it Comes to You

181

Traits and Attributes

➤ Although many people believe wolves are vicious, ruthless killers, quite the opposite is true. They are not known to attack humans and don't fight with each other unless there is no way to avoid it. Hungry wolves will kill livestock at times, but they generally prey on weak or sick animals, mostly small deer and rodents. Their hearing and sense of smell are highly developed. Extremely intelligent and social, wolves are playful and affectionate animals; they usually mate for life and are devoted to their families. These animals live by strict, ritualistic "codes of conduct" and subscribe to hierarchical social structures within their packs. Once common throughout North and Central America, a number of wolf species are now endangered.

People who have the wolf as their spirit helper often have a strong need for freedom, though they also respect authority. These individuals are gregarious and nurturing, holding family and tradition in high esteem. Some of them are quite adept at communication; many are very intuitive. Although wolf-people may possess great strength and endurance, they rarely engage in displays of bravado and are more likely to walk away from a fight than to provoke one.

Myths And Folklore About The Animal

➤ The Dakota believe that the wolf was the keeper of great knowledge, which it shares with humans through its "song" (howl). Many Native Americans hold the wolf in highest esteem as one of the last truly wild creatures. The Oglala connect the wolf with healing powers. The ancient Celts revered the wolf and viewed it as a symbol of spring. In Roman mythology, Romulus and Remus, twin brothers who founded Rome, were reared by a wolf mother.

Devotion to Family ◄

Loyalty

Intelligence

Traits You Can Borrow (Acquire) From This Spirit Animal

If you see a wolf, in its natural ◄
habitat or in a dream or other vision, it may
be signaling you to attend to family matters.
The wolf can also help you establish
priorities, stabilize your emotions, and keep
you from forming inappropriate
relationships. In some instances, it appears in
order to help you balance independence with
order and structure. At other times, Wolf
comes to encourage you to embrace your
"wild side."

What it Means if You See This Animal or if it Comes to You

WOODPECKER

Traits and Attributes

➤ This large bird with its characteristic red head is best known for rhythmically pecking on tree trunks with its sharp beak as it pursues insects for food. It moves up and down trees with its strong hooked claws using a peculiar forward and backward motion, and its up-and-down flight patterns are also unique. It is generally the male woodpecker who hollows out a space high in a tree where he builds a comfortable nest to provide shelter for the parent birds and their offspring. Woodpeckers are able to thrive in all climates and can be found in virtually every part of the world except Australia, New Zealand, Madagascar and the polar regions.

Myth's And Folklore About The Animal

People who have the woodpecker as their spirit helper are often blessed with natural rhythm. Individualistic and emotional, they march to the beat of a different drummer and are content to follow their own inner guidance. Once they've made up their minds, they can be very determined and methodical, probing deep into the heart of a matter to dig out answers. Like the bird itself, they cling tenaciously to their ideas, behaviors, possessions, the past, and loved ones. Intensely protective, woodpecker parents sometimes have trouble letting their children grow up to lead independent lives.

➤ Some Native Americans admired the woodpecker because its pecking sound was similar to the beat of a drum; others connected it with the heartbeat of the Earth. The Oglala believed that this bird foretold of storms and could enable human beings to talk to thunder. In Greek mythology, the woodpecker was the companion of the thunder god Zeus. The roman goddess Circe is said to have turned the god Picus into a woodpecker when he spurned her.

Resourcefulness ◄

Rhythmic Motion

Discrimination

If you see a woodpecker, in its ◄
natural habitat or in a dream or other vision,
it may suggest that you need to establish new
rhythms and patterns in your life. Or, it
might be encouraging you to follow your own
natural rhythms rather than trying to adjust
to the pace of the world around you. "Do
what's best for you," is Woodpecker's message.

A SPECIAL PROMISE

Marc Brinkerhoff's animal kingdom illustrations hold a special promise for you. They possess qualities like no others you have seen before. They reflect his love and compassion for all of the animals brought to you in this book. As a psychic, Marc is intimately connected to animals as individuals. He knows how they think and how they see us. He also has the ability to put you in touch with them in a very special way. Each picture is imbued with feelings. Just gazing at them promises to evoke the same heart-felt emotions and communications Marc experienced as he created them.

You are encouraged to spend time looking at each animal until a sense of familiarity wells up from within you. Thus, you will initiate some unique and rewarding friendships with these spirit animal helpers.